GW01417676

Quality

THE PERFECT SERIES

ALL YOU NEED TO GET IT RIGHT FIRST TIME

OTHER TITLES IN THE SERIES:

Perfect Quality

ALL YOU NEED
TO GET IT RIGHT
FIRST TIME

BRYN OWEN

A

ARROW
BUSINESS BOOKS

Published by Arrow Books in 1995

1 3 5 7 9 10 8 6 4 2

© Bryn Owen 1995

Bryn Owen has asserted his rights under the Copyright, Designs and Patents Act, 1988 to be identified as the author of this work.

This book is sold subject to the condition that it shall not, by way of trade or otherwise, be lent, resold, hired out or otherwise circulated without the publisher's prior consent in any form of binding or cover other than that in which it is published and without a similar condition including this condition being imposed on the subsequent purchaser.

First published by
Arrow Books Limited
20 Vauxhall Bridge Road, London SW1V 2SA

Random House Australia (Pty) Limited
20 Alfred Street, Milsons Point, Sydney
New South Wales 2061, Australia

Random House New Zealand Limited
18 Poland Road, Glenfield
Auckland 10, New Zealand

Random House South Africa (Pty) Limited
PO Box 337, Bergvlei, South Africa

Papers used by Random House UK Limited are natural, recyclable products made from wood grown in sustainable forests. The manufacturing processes conform to the environmental regulations of the country of origin.

Random House UK Limited Reg. No. 954009

ISBN 0 09 955611 1

Set in Bembo by
SX Composing Ltd, Rayleigh, Essex
Printed and bound in Great Britain by
Cox and Wyman Ltd, Reading, Berks

British Library Cataloguing in Publication Data
A catalogue record for this book is available from
the British Library

ABOUT THE AUTHOR

Bryn Owen, BSc, MSc, PhD, DMS, CEng, FIEE, FIQA, FAQMC

Now in his third career, Bryn Owen started work over 30 years ago as a Production Engineer. During the following 15 years he worked in manufacturing industry in the UK and Nigeria. His posts included five years as Plant Manager of a domestic appliance factory and six years as Quality Manager in the automotive industry. Before becoming a full time consultant in 1986 he was the Head of Computer Aided Engineering at Salford University College. There he was responsible for the development and presentation of courses in the field of Quality.

Bryn has written two books on achieving ISO 9000 registration. The first of these books describes in everyday language the findings of his research for which he was awarded a PhD in 1991. This work involved the development of a model to simplify the design of the optimum quality system. Workshops based on his work have been run in the USA, Europe, the Middle East and the Far East.

Bryn believes that education and training must be lifelong, for the individual, employer and society. He actively encourages others to develop themselves and their staff through his work as an Open University Tutor and a non-executive Director of his local Training and Enterprise Council.

Bryn Owen is currently Chief Executive of Optimum Systems for Quality, a firm of quality consultants who have worked with many clients to improve their quality systems. The company has an international reputation for quality and has clients throughout the UK, in the USA and the Middle East. To demonstrate their progress down the road of continual improvement Optimum Systems has achieved registration to ISO 9001 and Investors in People.

The objective of this book is to build an awareness in the readers of the necessity to pursue quality and to show the benefits that follow. If you want further guidance along the road to quality, then Bryn can be contacted at Optimum Systems via the telephone, 01282-779002 or fax 01282-779099.

Dr Bryn Owen

CONTENTS

ACKNOWLEDGMENTS

Quality is concerned with providing customers with a performance that is perceived to give value. This is rarely achieved by working alone, but through teams of individuals with shared objectives. This has certainly been the case with this book and I gladly acknowledge the help and assistance given by all who have contributed to its contents.

My thoughts on quality have been influenced by writers who have published on the subject, but more importantly by discussions with those people who, day by day, consider what quality means to them. These discussions have been in everyday life and during thirty years working in industry, commerce and education. This text draws on discussions and experiences from throughout that period. I thank the many colleagues and clients who have developed my thinking and have provided the anecdotes in this book.

The team of individuals who have helped me most during the task of preparing the manuscript are my colleagues at Optimum Systems for Quality. They have discussed and reviewed the contents and worked with me to improve the content. This editing team has included Claire Huckin, Christine Lowe, Mel Owen, Ed Payne and Steve Rowe. They say that one picture is worth a thousand words and so a special thanks goes to Allen Leaver for his excellent work in preparing the illustrations.

FOREWORD

Quality, especially with regard to ISO 9000, has become the latest media casualty, and like most such casualties, this is the result of mis-reporting and ignorance. Bryn Owen's book makes the case for Quality Assurance in business and commerce being as important as oxygen is to life iself. It is in fact a breath of fresh air, and underpins the importance of the subject. Every executive and line manager should have a copy, if only to remind them of the fundamentals.

Peter Nicholson, The Nicholson Partnership

INTRODUCTION

The achievement of Quality is a major issue throughout industry, commerce and government bodies. It is not just a passing craze or the flavour of the month. It is at the heart of the success of every business. It is vital for survival and growth.

We have been blessed with some excellent 'prophets' who have developed many approaches and techniques to improve quality. These people have proved that a sustained and scientific drive towards quality can make significant differences to the standard of performance of an organisation and hence to its profits. Their work has transformed companies, industries and indeed countries.

We have been cursed with many false 'prophets' who claim to be knowledgeable and are yet barely able to understand the essentials. They have become 'experts' through seeing one or two techniques used in specific circumstances. They ply their trade and their followers achieve little except high bills, poorly trained staff and badly documented systems.

To understand how to achieve quality it is essential that you have a clear understanding of what is meant by quality, why it is essential, who is responsible and when it is achieved. Most people know when they are pleased with what they have delivered and received, but to describe what this comprises is not an easy task. This book considers quality in non-technical terms, and presents a text which answers the What, Why, Who, How and When of Quality.

Everywhere there is more and more emphasis on

quality. League tables, Citizens' Charters and Quality Policies all try to set standards and indicate performance. Many of these miss the real meaning of quality; most of them, on their own, do little to improve it.

If quality is to be achieved it has to become the way of life for all. Everyone must be committed and involved. It cannot be left to quality experts. They cannot achieve quality, their role is to ensure that others understand and live quality.

Perfect Quality is intended to start the process of learning that will transform the reader's thinking on quality. It is suitable for both those who must lead the process and those involved in the process, in the public and private sectors, in manufacturing and service industries. All should be concerned with quality; all need to know about quality.

There are many techniques and standards associated with quality. These are tools to be used with care by people with an understanding of when they are applicable and when they can add value. They do not achieve quality. When properly applied they provide the means to achieve quality. Their relevance and use is described in this book, but the teaching of these techniques is beyond its scope.

Quality means giving customers a product or service that they perceive is of value to them. If the customer is delighted then quality is achieved. This book is intended to delight its readers and if the principles in it are followed then they should be able to add value to the service they provide.

1
WHAT IS QUALITY?

SUMMARY

The awareness of quality has never been greater in industry, commerce and government than it is today. It is used as one of the criteria to judge the service provided by private companies and public bodies, but the real meaning of quality is often lost.

To achieve quality it is necessary to ensure that agreed requirements are met, but quality is far more than meeting requirements. Quality, by its very nature, is about ensuring that every aspect of the product or service is of a standard that delights the customer and provides value to the customer.

This does not imply excellence at any cost. Cost is clearly part of the achievement of quality, and customers do not expect more than they are paying for. They do expect, and are entitled to receive, products and services that are of value to them. If this is not achieved, they will rightly complain and go elsewhere.

Customers' expectations are continually changing. What they were pleased with yesterday, they will complain about tomorrow. To achieve quality consistently it is necessary to research and anticipate their needs.

Quality is difficult to define, but what is sure is that we all know when it is achieved and when it is not. This assessment is subjective and will vary from individual to individual and from occasion to occasion. To be successful, businesses must make this assessment for themselves and then ensure that they achieve quality.

QUALITY – A PHILOSOPHICAL CONCEPT

Quality is not something we can see, touch, taste or hear, and yet whenever we do these things we assess the quality of the sensation we perceive. We all make this assessment, but we may not all agree on the results. Quality is not mind or matter, but our perception of it is influenced by what we experience and what we think.

While we may not agree on what constitutes quality, we have a common idea of what it involves. We all accept that it is concerned with high standards and excellence rather than inferior performance and failure, but may not agree on what constitutes a high standard or an inferior performance. A standard that pleases one, offends another.

Quality is subjective, and it is because of this that it is difficult to gain agreement. What is certain is that whenever we part with money, we expect quality in return. This is true in our personal lives as well as in business.

What we expect is coloured by how much money we are paying. If we are paying £25,000 for a new car, we expect a higher level of quality than if we are only paying £5,000. In both cases we expect the car to operate, but our detailed expectations are different.

A recent customer survey found that the purchasers of a particular make of cheap imported car reported the highest level of satisfaction with their purchase. They had paid little and expected little, and were pleased with the result. They were satisfied customers and perceived that they had made a quality purchase. Others in the survey had paid more and expected more, and some of these were dissatisfied with a 'better' car.

If we expect to receive quality, then we should expect to have to provide quality – quality as assessed by our customers. To achieve this we need to take the subjectivity out of the equation and establish a level of performance which is understood and accepted.

QUALITY – FITNESS FOR PURPOSE

In an attempt to establish a working definition of quality, an early quality guru, Dr Joseph Juran, defined quality as that which is fit for its purpose. This clearly removes some subjectivity, as it is often easy to establish what is fit for the purpose. A light bulb that fits and works is fit for its purpose. A light bulb that fits and does not work is not fit for its purpose.

It does, however, beg the question of 'whose purpose?' This was addressed by Plato in his theory of art; over two thousand years ago he concluded that it was the customer who defined the purpose, the customer who defined the quality level.

While this definition removes some subjectivity, it introduces the problem of deciding what is the purpose. This is clearly a prerequisite to the use of the definition, and as it is the purpose the customer defines it still involves customer satisfaction.

As a definition, Fitness for Purpose is mechanistic in nature. It is useful to define the more measurable aspects of the purpose, but falls down on the more ephemeral aspects.

It is difficult to arrive at a 'purpose' of a car that includes all of the aesthetic and comfort aspects expected by purchasers. The purpose of a car is to transport people in safety and comfort. A car with a paint blemish can achieve this, but clearly this would detract from the satisfaction of the customer, and so would detract from quality.

This can be addressed by defining more closely the purpose of the car to include all aspects of its design. It is possible to define that to be fit for purpose the paintwork has to be free from blemishes. If care isn't taken,

3

the next argument becomes when is a mark a blemish, and is a blemish on the bonnet as important as a blemish inside the boot lid!

Another problem with the fitness for purpose definition is that the purpose may not always be known. A manufacturer of light bulbs may make two models, one model designed to last 1,000 hours for domestic use and another to last 10,000 hours for industrial purposes. This again leads to a need to closely define what is being offered. Quality is then ensuring what is offered is what is delivered – quality becomes Conformance to the Requirements.

QUALITY – CONFORMANCE TO THE REQUIREMENTS

A widely-used definition of quality in industry is Conformance to Requirements. This definition is often attributed to Philip Crosby, another well-known guru of quality. The definition places emphasis on the need to meet the specification, and any deviation from this is a reduction in quality. In these terms quality is meeting specifications and making it right first time. A 1,000-hour light bulb made to specification and a 10,000-hour light bulb made to a higher specification are both quality light bulbs.

This definition requires precise specifications based on research and development. It leads to an emphasis on the reliability of the product or service. All characteristics of the product or service need to be defined, as it is no longer permissible to allow for local decisions to be made based on fitness for use.

In practice this has led to a high level of detailed specifications defining the finish required and the way in which this is to be assessed – specifications, for instance, that indicate when a paint blemish is a blemish, and where it is and is not acceptable.

The Government-inspired Citizens' Charters are attempts to define the requirements of a good service. Generally these Charters have defined the acceptable times for services to be provided, and this does provide an easily measurable parameter by which the service can be assessed.

Defining all the features and characteristics of the product or service which is to be supplied can be a mammoth task. The cost of undertaking it can far outweigh the benefits gained. They standardize service, but customers are not standard and a standardized service is not always in line with their requirements.

A brewery, in an attempt to improve service, introduced training for its bar staff in all its pubs. They decided the most appropriate greeting as customers arrived and trained the staff accordingly.

The day after the training a regular came into one pub and instead of being greeted with the normal 'Half of mild is it Harold?' he was faced with 'Good evening sir, what would you like to drink tonight?' The personal touch had been replaced by a standard service, but was it a high standard of service?

The Conformance to Requirements definition is even more mechanistic than Fitness for Purpose with black-white specifications removing the need for subjectivity. Quality becomes a matter of getting the details defined and then ensuring they are achieved, and achieved all of the time, every time. There is a clear danger that the individual
customer becomes less important than the standard.

With Conformance to Requirements little is left to

interpretation, the standard requirement is clearly pre-
scribed. Defining requirements and ensuring conformance may be a part of quality, but quality is more than
this.

QUALITY – ZERO DEFECTS

Conformance to requirements provides standards, the
achievement of which can be verified. With clear requirements it is easy to decide when quality has not
been achieved, and little is left to interpretation. The
question is then posed regarding the frequency at which
management will permit the specification not to be
met. What is a realistic target for achieving perfection?

Philip Crosby clearly saw that there was only one
acceptable level of performance and that was perfection, to specification every time, all of the time. The
phrase 'Zero Defects' (ZD) was coined to describe this
performance standard.

With Zero Defects any failure to meet the defined requirement is considered a defect. This definition is in
effect the same as Conformance to Requirements, but it
has been used to launch Zero Defects Campaigns.

Zero Defect Campaigns are used to focus everyone's
attention on quality. They promote the idea that everyone should be aiming to achieve Zero Defects in all that
they do. Any deviation from this absolute standard is a
failure in performance, a failure in quality. Emphasis is
placed on process control to segregate any deviations
from specification early in the process, and Zero
Defects is the objective.

When the Zero Defect objective is not achieved there is
a loss due to the imperfection. This loss has been used
by a leading Japanese quality guru, Taguchi, as the basis
for his definition of quality. He defined the loss due to

any imperfection as the 'negative quality' of the product or service – the larger the deviation, the larger the loss and the lower the quality. As the loss can be quantified, all be it with much difficulty, it becomes possible to quantify the quality.

QUALITY – DELIGHTING THE CUSTOMER

The Fitness for Purpose, Conformance to Require-ments and Zero Defects definitions of quality are customer-focused. They seek to establish a level of performance that is acceptable to customers, a quality level that ensures that customers' needs are met and that they have no cause to complain.

It is true that if this level of performance is not achieved, then quality is not achieved. Is this the same as saying the achievement of the acceptable is the achievement of quality?

A driver who drives home without breaking the law is not necessarily a quality driver. A golf player who completes a round without breaking the rules is not necessarily a quality player. Failure to obey the rules would suggest a lack of quality, but mere conformance does not provide quality.

There is a level of performance, which if exceeded, will result in a customer who becomes committed to the supplier. A customer who is committed is one who comes back, who tells others of our performance, who values us. It is a customer we value and a customer to whom we provide value.

That level of performance is above the level required to meet the specification or to provide a performance that is fit for purpose. Between these two levels there is a 'grey' area, a range of levels of performance where the specifications are achieved, but the customers are not committed; where they do not complain, but do not feel they have really gained value. If a business operates in this area is it providing quality, or is it just providing satisfaction?

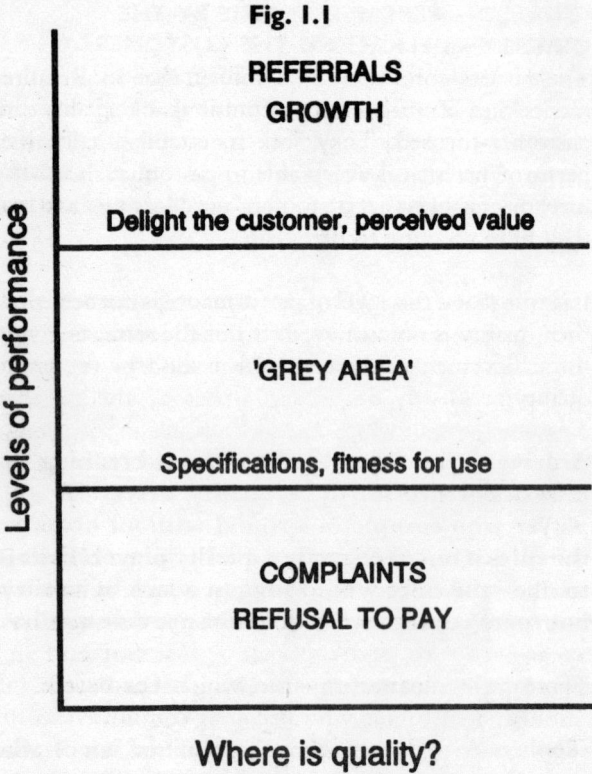

Fig. 1.1

REFERRALS
GROWTH

Delight the customer, perceived value

'GREY AREA'

Specifications, fitness for use

COMPLAINTS
REFUSAL TO PAY

Levels of performance

Where is quality?

In its full meaning quality is far more than conformance, far more than fitness for purpose. Quality is concerned with providing a service that delights our customers. This is the definition promoted by Dr Edward Deming, considered by many to be the ultimate quality guru. He maintained that satisfying a customer is not enough. This may prevent complaints, but a satisfied customer may go elsewhere for his next purchase. To ensure repeat business and loyal customers it is necessary to provide a performance that delights the customer.

QUALITY – PERCEIVED VALUE BY THE CUSTOMER

Customers are only delighted when their expectations are exceeded, when they perceive that they have received more value from the transaction than anticipated. This is the level of performance that shows that quality has been achieved, but establishing that level still involves subjectivity.

Expectations vary from customer to customer, occasion to occasion and are continually increasing with time. They include not just the product or the service being provided, but every aspect of the supplier-customer relationship, indeed shortfalls in the product or service may be accepted if other aspects of the relationship excel.

When out on a cold day for a walk in the hills a cup of hot coffee from a wayside caravan, which was not anticipated, may be a delight. It does not have to be espresso or cappuccino, just hot and in a reasonably clean mug – the bigger the better.

That same day, after a meal in an Italian restaurant, a perfectly made cup of coffee is what you expect. That in itself will not delight. Even the mint chocolates have become expected, and their absence is more likely to cause dissatisfaction than their presence bring delight.

There is a point at which the price of the mug of coffee may be high enough to ruin the delight. It is unlikely, even if the coffee in the restaurant was

free, that this, by itself, would create delight, yet price is clearly a factor in deciding what creates delight so the price paid clearly influences the perception of quality.

Quality is the level of performance that delights the customer. This is achieved when the customer's perception of the transaction is that value has been gained. This value is not just about money, but every aspect of the relationship between the supplier and the customer.

Customers perceive value not just in monetary terms. Value can be perceived through the care given and through the interest paid. Providing more is not the same as providing value, it can even have the opposite effect.

Extra large portions of food which cannot be eaten can be seen as wasteful and detract from the perceived value of a meal. There is a limit to how long people will wait even for the cheapest bargain. Staff who know nothing about the products add no value, but knowledgeable staff can ensure the customer makes the right choice for the customer, not the supplier.

To provide value you have to value the customers and treat them accordingly. Without them there is no business. They are the reason for the existence of the business and to keep them they need to value what you do, they need to be delighted with your performance.

If the customer perceives that value has been provided, that he values the deal in all its aspects, then quality has been provided. This is the level of performance that has to be found by the supplier if he wants to know what quality means to him. This is the level of performance that has to be planned for by the supplier if he aims to achieve quality. This is the level of performance that has to be assured if quality is to be achieved.

QUALITY – ACHIEVING TOTAL QUALITY

Alongside the development of the meaning of quality has been the idea of Total Quality which some see as synonymous with quality. Total Quality, Total Quality Management (TQM), Total Quality Control (TQC), Quality Improvement Programme (QIP), and Company Wide Quality Improvement (CWQI), are some of the many terms used to promote and express this concept.

In essence, Total Quality is an acceptance that for quality to be achieved it has to be recognized that the pursuit of quality is an integral part of the whole business. Quality has to be incorporated into all departments, it has to be considered in all decisions, the pursuit of quality has to become the way of life of the business.

There is no simple, commonly accepted definition of Total Quality, or even agreement on what it involves. Many writers and consultancies have generated their own title, with associated definitions, and often have a defined methodology for achieving it, but there is no clear agreement.

Total Quality Management (TQM) is defined in a British Standard, BS 7850 : Part 1 : 1992 as : –

'Management philosophy and company practices that aim to harness the human and material resources of an organisation in the most effective way to achieve the objectives of the organisation.'

While this definition does not specifically mention quality it shows that Total Quality deals with the central beliefs, concerns and operational culture of an organization. It aims to focus everyone on the improvement of quality, from the boardroom to the shopfloor, from the council chamber to the traffic warden. It recognizes that all have a role to play in achieving quality and all need to be motivated, trained and developed to fulfil that role. This requires an emphasis throughout the whole organization on continually and systematically seeking out ways to improve quality, rather than slavishly pursuing turnover and output. This generally requires a major transformation in management thinking and actions.

Kaizen is the Japanese word for continuous and gradual improvement over time and this embodies the Japanese approach to Total Quality. The Kaizen approach is to seek perpetual change and improvement of every phase of the business by everyone in the business. It involves challenging and improving the existing standard rather than striving to reach a standard.

QUALITY – CONCERN FOR INTERNAL CUSTOMERS

Most employees in businesses have no contact with customers. Their work does not easily allow them to learn the customers' requirements and it may seem to have little to do with the customers. What does quality mean to them? How can they be involved in delighting customers when they never meet them?

The idea of looking at others in the business as internal customers has been evolved to overcome this problem. It recognizes that everyone has a role to play in achieving quality. In this concept everyone in an organization can consider their relationships with other members of the organization on the basis of customer–supplier.

At the simplest level in a production environment the

next operator down the assembly line is your customer. Your performance should delight that customer; it should be perceived as being of value. Similarly you are the customer of the operators who feed work to you. Their work should be perceived as valuable to you.

This is similarly true in office environments. The sales office clerk is the customer of the sales representative who sends orders into the office. That sales representative must supply quality if the relationship is to have value. The order must be clearly and completely recorded so that it can be processed efficiently. That makes a quality performance in that relationship. A quality performance can be critical to the business being able to provide quality to the external customer.

In many businesses the analysis of relationships as supplier–customer links becomes complex. When giving a handwritten letter to a secretary to be typed, the secretary is the customer of the boss. When the letter has been typed and returned, the boss is the customer of the secretary.

This complexity does not detract from the value of the idea and its use in achieving quality. If we all consider transactions as supplier–customer relationships and seek to provide quality to our internal customers, then overall, quality will improve. If we accept that to improve we need to know how we are performing, then we should seek out information on our own performance and seek to improve it.

These customer–supplier links in a business are often shown as links in a chain, the quality chain. Each individual in the chain is considered to be a link, and the overall strength of the chain is dependent on the weakest link. This illustration shows how quality can be lost by just one weak link.

Fig. 1.2

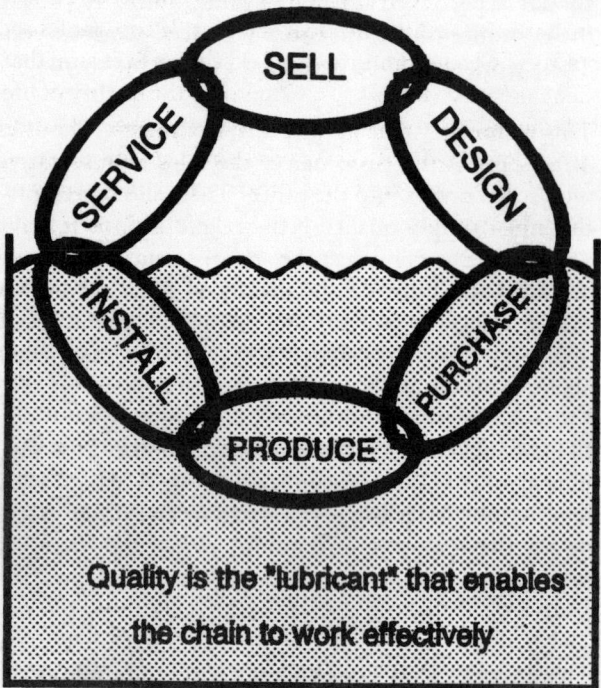

SELL

SERVICE

DESIGN

INSTALL

PURCHASE

PRODUCE

Quality is the "lubricant" that enables
the chain to work effectively

The Quality Chain

Quality is achieved by the whole chain functioning
efficiently. When there is friction between links, quality
must be the lubrication to make the links run smoothly
again.

The quality chain links all of the business, and its external suppliers, to providing quality to the final, external, customer. That is the objective of the business
and can only be achieved if each link provides quality.

QUALITY – THE OBJECTIVE OF BUSINESS, AND FOR BUSINESS

The quality of life in any society is dependent on how it produces goods and provides services. If companies set out to find the minimum standard that will ensure that their customers do not complain, then the quality of life will stagnate. If they set out to ensure that their customers are delighted with their performance, and perceive that they have received value from it, then the quality of life will improve.

For society to improve the quality of life of its members, industry, commerce and government require a definition of quality that promotes this drive. This definition must reflect the full meaning of quality, and not diminish it to mere conformance. It must be a definition that reflects the full meaning of quality, a definition that not only provides what is needed, but helps to develop customer needs by providing more value, and delighting the customer with the result.

The determination of what is fit for the purpose, and the establishment of standards to define what is required, are steps on the way to providing value to the customer. In themselves they are not quality, but are useful in the achievement of quality.

Once a business has committed itself to quality then it needs to establish the level of performance that will delight its customers, that they perceive will give them value. This level of performance is fit for that purpose, but it is a continually changing level. It must not become the new definition of quality, but part of the route to implement quality.

When it is known what is fit for the purpose this can be defined in formal requirements, in specifications and standards. Conformance to these is necessary, but they must be continually reviewed to confirm they are fit for the purpose of delighting the customer and providing perceived value.

Quality is about continual improvement, about using each setback, each shortfall, as an opportunity to seek ways to improve. To continually provide quality – a performance that delights and provides value – a business has to use all of its resources. Total Quality can only be achieved by total commitment and understanding throughout the whole business, all the time. This approach to Total Quality will ensure the cost of quality is minimized and provide a high quality of life for customers and employees alike.

2

WHY IS QUALITY VITAL TO SURVIVAL?

SUMMARY

Every time we part with money we expect quality in return. This is equally true for the individual in the high street and the corporate buyer negotiating major contracts. We expect quality, if we do not receive it we go elsewhere.

Quality is vital to keep existing customers and to find new ones, so it has to be a priority in the competitive environment of today. The choice available to all buyers has never been greater as international trade has become simpler, and locally the competition is often intense.

It is often thought that achieving quality costs more, but the facts do not bear this out. In fact it is failure to achieve quality that costs industry an estimated 20 per cent of its turnover. Every time something needs correcting, is scrapped or re-worked it costs more, and these extra costs far outweigh the cost of achieving quality. If they are reduced or eliminated then the cost of the operation reduces. It is always cheaper to do it right first time!

When things are only done once, capacity that was previously wasted is available. Morale is no longer upset by having to repeat work and everyone sees the value of their contribution.

QUALITY, THE BEST ROUTE TO KEEPING CUSTOMERS

A well–satisfied customer is one who continues to buy from you. They treat you as their preferred supplier and often do not consider using others. They are the best customers you can have. If you look after them, they will look after you. They do not require massive advertising campaigns and sales drives. They do require good products, good service, good communications and consideration. In short they require quality.

A business that is built on loyal customers is a good business. Loyal customers are an asset, and are even shown on a balance sheet as 'Goodwill'. It may take years to develop a sound customer base, and customers need to be valued. They deserve to be taken seriously and to be listened to, since without them there is no business.

It is determining and meeting their needs profitably that has to be the first objective of every business. If that objective is not met, then decline is inevitable.

Keeping customers is not just about providing the same good service today and every day. Customer expectations change. They change because of new technology and competition. What was considered to be a luxury yesterday is a necessity tomorrow. If you do not anticipate changes and meet them, then you are not providing quality to your customers. If you do not provide quality then you will lose your customers.

The purchasing manager started to analyse the reject items found on incoming goods. These were returned to the suppliers and credit was gained, but handling them was time-consuming and disrupted the flow of materials to the factory.

When the suppliers came to talk about price increases they were presented with the information and it was made clear that price rises would be dependent on improvements in quality.

Your customers are your life blood. You have to understand and be responsive to their demands. You need to listen to what they are saying and examine whether you can improve the products and services you provide. If they bother to tell you something, then you must listen and understand their point of view. You might not agree, but it is essential that you understand so that you can decide the appropriate response.

But it is not sufficient to respond to your customers' current demands. Your competitors will be taking pro-active steps to win them away. They will be going out to find out who they are, what they really want, how your product or service fails to meet their needs and expectations. They will be developing plans to improve and offer something better.

You need to do the same. They are your customers, but you cannot take them for granted. They will switch if they think you are indifferent to their needs, particularly if the alternative suppliers appear more responsive. It is no good saying to a customer when he has gone elsewhere that you could have met his requirements if only he had asked. The competition asked and you didn't.

A fish merchant supplied fresh fish to all the chip shops in a large town. He ensured that they all had fresh supplies by delivering each morning fish that had come from the docks earlier that day. His refrigerated vans made the deliveries well before the shops opened, often leaving the fish before the owners arrived.

Suddenly, he found that he had lost most of his customers to a competitor. When he investigated he discovered that this company had spoken to the owners and discovered that they would prefer the fish delivered in the afternoon when they were there and could meet the driver and take the delivery straight into the chiller.

He could have provided that service, but he never bothered to find out what his customers wanted. He assumed that the way he operated suited them. They never complained, they probably would never have thought about a change in the service, but the competitor did.

You may know that your product and service is of a higher quality, but it is your customers' perception of your quality that counts. You need to be convincing them that you are the best by exploring with them ways in which you can improve.

So quality goes right through the organization. Market research, design and development are all part of the drive to provide quality. They all have a role to play. They need to be part of the quality system, the system that sets out to provide quality to customers.

Customers do not require perfection to remain loyal, but they do expect any complaints to be effectively and quickly resolved. Your systems need to encourage your customers to let you know when they are not happy. That is vital information to enable you to retain your customers.

Customers who are not satisfied with your perform-ance will not always complain. They will just go else-where and never come back. They might tell their friends and colleagues, but often they cannot handle the stress and conflict involved in telling you. That does not mean you can afford to ignore them. You need to have staff and systems that draw out their opinions, that value their complaints and respond to them. Unless you find out what they perceive as wrong, you lose the opportunity to improve.

Research indicates that among those who are not

happy and don't complain, over 90 per cent do not come back. Among those who do complain and have their complaints resolved quickly over 80 per cent return.

To keep your customers you have to provide quality, and that means a standard of service and product that totally meets their needs and exceeds their expectations. Expectations change, and you should determine the changes, and as far as possible be pro-active in leading the changes. That is what quality is about.

QUALITY, THE BEST ROUTE TO GAINING CUSTOMERS

The best new customers are the ones who come to you because of references. They have been told how good you are and want to do business with you, it's just a matter of agreeing the terms. References only come as a result of a quality performance, a performance that delights the receiver.

To win references you need to convince your current customers that you are the best. They will not give a good reference unless they have been convinced, and that means providing quality.

Some references will just come naturally. People talk about their own experiences and others listen. It may be a casual conversation about where to go for a good meal, or more formal enquiries from colleagues in the same industry. All of these can bring valuable new customers, customers that help your business to grow.

My local hardware store is a long-established, tra- ditional shop stocking everything from seeds to china, from paint to suitcases. It is staffed by people who know their products and their uses. If they cannot help, then they point you to someone

who can. **There are several nearby hardware chainstores which claim to stock everything and compete on price, but the local shop competes on expertise, variety and service – in other words on quality.**

Some time ago the plastic facing on my penknife came loose and I went to the local store and asked advice on the most suitable adhesive to repair it. I was given informed advice and made my purchase.

Later, I realized that I had left my penknife on the shop counter. I went back to recover it and found to my delight that it had been repaired! The assistant concerned was not in sight, but I wrote to the owners to tell them about the service and I frequently recommend them to others. They had truly delighted me, they had provided quality.

It is not necessary to wait for references. If you think you provide quality, then it is worth checking this out with your customers. Talk to them about your performance, and if they are delighted ask them for references. Ask them if they know of others who might need your products or services. Solicit their opinions through questionnaires on your performance. Use these references when approaching potential customers.

Registration to quality standards can be a valuable way to distinguish you from the competition. This can be particularly valuable in one–off service industries where it is difficult to assess quality before selecting a supplier. Estate agents are typical of a service which has a poor reputation and is difficult to assess. While pleasant surroundings and staff contribute to quality, a certificate confirming a quality system can provide a potential client with an indication that you have addressed quality and are taking it seriously.

Eventually, references lead to reputation. A reputation of being a quality firm is a sure way to gain customers. Often the basis of the reputation is unknown, or may indeed be outdated, but it lasts. It is a valuable asset and brings customers, but if quality is not achieved the reputation can soon be lost. It is often said that you are only as good as your last job. That may not be totally true as loyal customers will forgive, but it is certainly easier to lose a reputation than to regain it.

Most of the British motor industry lost its reputation for quality in the 1970s. The competition from more reliable Japanese cars resulted in factories being closed and marques disappearing.

Once lost the reputation was only regained by addressing quality seriously. Improvements through learning from the Japanese has allowed this to happen and now cars made in Britain are once again seen as being of good quality.

Concentration on quality is essential to gain new customers. Every satisfied customer is a good advertisement, but a delighted customer is the best advertisement you can have.

Dr Edward Deming writes that 'It will not suffice to have customers that are merely satisfied. An unhappy customer will switch. Unfortunately, a satisfied customer may also switch, on the theory that he could not lose much, and might gain. Profit in business comes from repeat customers, customers that boast about your products and service, and that bring friends with them.'

QUALITY, THE BEST ROUTE TO REDUCING COSTS

It is usually assumed that quality costs money. It is often said that 'Yes we want quality, but we cannot afford it' or 'the customers will not pay for it'. Nothing could be further from the truth. It is the failure to achieve quality that costs money – through scrap, rework, late deliveries and warranty. All of these add to the cost of running a business, and in the final analysis all have to be passed on to the customer.

The failure to achieve a quality service first time, every time, results in things having to be done again. This is as true in the office as on the factory floor. When poor verbal or written communications result in confusion, quality suffers.

Most companies know the value of their turnover or profit. Given some time they can normally find the cost of wages and purchases. Ask them the cost of quality and they rarely know.

Even in organizations where scrap and re-work are recorded, it is unusual to find that these figures are reported to senior management. Often they are just accepted as part of the operation of a business. Some companies expect scrap, so they grow to accept it as normal. They issue enough material for 110 pieces when they only want 100, and expect ten to be scrapped. They build it into their costings, and just absorb it – or rather let their profits absorb it.

When a textile factory was preparing its budgets it included an allowance for scrap of five per cent. They had found that this was a realistic figure for their processes as it took account of faults in the material and wastage at the end of rolls. They needed to budget for these occurrences to ensure they would make a profit.

They used the budget to create the plan as they wanted consistent figures across the company.

**They included the scrap allowance in the Produc-
tion Planning System. Whenever they issued an
order for products they issued five per cent more
material than they theoretically needed – they
planned to scrap one in 20 items.**

**On occasions things went well and there were no
problems with the cloth and the factory beat the
budget. They then had extra products which the
computer system could not accept – it believed it
was impossible to make more than the plan. The
supervisors then had to fiddle the system to make
it accept the surplus. They had been set a target of
making five per cent scrap and it was easier for
them if they scrapped the items!**

The target has to be zero defects. The budgets can be
based on the present level of performance, but to ask
people to aim for failure condones and encourages it.

The cost of quality is not confined to your own
organization. If purchasing is a significant part of your
operations the quality costs of your suppliers are inevitably built into your costs.

Service companies and departments often do not even
think in terms of scrap. Just have a look in the waste bin
in any office and find out how many documents were
produced and then scrapped. It's not the cost of the
paper that is significant, but the time taken to check,
correct and re-print. Typists and secretaries often have
to produce the same letter three or four times before it is
accepted – with reports it can be even more. Often this
is not down to their performance, but to the author's
poor handwriting or changes in the content or format.
This is just as much scrap and rework as making faulty
items on the factory floor.

Mistakes in the office have a disproportionate effect on

the costs of manufacture. One wrong dimension on a drawing can result in the factory making parts that do not fit. A poorly written figure on an order can result in the factory making and delivering the wrong product.

A manufacturer of beds supplied three standard widths, three feet, four feet six inches and five feet. The sales representatives recorded the sizes and quantity required on standard order forms which were sent to the factory.

Unfortunately there were problems with handwriting. Figure threes were often mistaken for fives, and vice versa. Once the order was entered it was processed right through to the customer and it was not until the actual delivery of the beds that the error was discovered.

The form was redesigned to replace the writing of the size with ticking boxes. This eliminated the possibility of error.

This illustrates an important relationship between mistakes in the office and mistakes in the factory. If there is an error on an order and everyone works with the erroneous data, then the chances are that it will not be found until it is delivered to the customer. If the error occurs in the development of the specification, then it may not be apparent until final test. If the error is in the detailed design then it becomes apparent during assembly, but if the error is made in the factory then it is generally quickly found and dealt with.

A major engineering company decided to determine the cost of quality in the design department. A representative sample of the modifications to designs was selected and analysed to determine whether the changes were the result of a change in

requirements or to correct an error. From this analysis the time taken correcting errors on designs, after they had been released to production, was found. It came out at 20 per cent.

20 per cent of the cost of the design function was being wasted because they had not got it right first time. In addition to the cost in the design function is the knock-on effect on production. They suffered from the errors in design and manufactured parts that did not fit or would not function correctly. All of these costs were part of the quality cost of the organization; all of these costs added to the cost of the products; all of the costs reduced the profits.

The majority of companies who do not know their cost of quality find when they measure it that it is around 20 per cent of the turnover. In some industries it can be as high as 30 per cent.

Many Japanese companies, who take the measurement of the cost of quality as part of the normal practice in running a business, have quality costs of less than one per cent. This is impressive, and it is certainly good to know it is achievable. By taking the measurement of quality costs seriously, and setting targets to reduce them, it is generally possible to drive them down to two or three per cent of sales turnover within a reasonable time.

The resultant savings of over 15 per cent of turnover go straight on to the bottom line. A reduction in scrap and rework results in an addition to profit. There is nowhere else for the figure to go. What does that do to the profit? In many cases it increases three, four or even five fold.

The cost of quality is not just the cost of doing things

wrong the first time. Generally it is still necessary to deliver the product or service. The original plan is no longer viable and other measures are needed. These may be working overtime, using express carriers, hiring temporary labour or sub-contracting work out. All of these necessitate extra costs, costs that were not included in the original budget. These extra costs are part of the cost of quality.

A company manufacturing plastic mouldings had a full order book and the factory was fully loaded. Christmas was approaching and they had a target number of items to ship to customers. Unfortunately 20 per cent of the items produced that month were not of the required quality.

The customers needed the shipments for continuity of their own work. The only way to meet these commitments was for the factory to work overtime making new items. They had to open and heat the factory during the planned shut down, pay premium rates to the operators and deliver the items using express delivery services.

What was the cost of not achieving the required quality level the first time?

Quality does not cost more. Finding the quality costs, analysing them and setting targets to reduce them is the route to reducing costs. The cost of quality is a latent gold mine in most companies. Find out what the figures are, find out why they exist, develop and implement plans to reduce them. This is the way forward, the way to make money out of quality.

QUALITY, THE BEST ROUTE TO INCREASING CAPACITY

Poor quality not only increases the cost, it results in a loss of capacity. If an average of 20 per cent of industry's time is being spent correcting and reworking, then there is at least 20 per cent latent capacity for additional work.

This latent capacity may be present in any function – sales, administration, purchasing, design or production. It provides the potential for an organization to increase output without increasing costs, or to maintain the same output and reduce the operating costs.

A sales director estimated that half of the sales calls made by his sales team were to deal with customer complaints. They prided themselves that they handled them well – often by giving discounts or new deliveries. They felt that the business did not unduly suffer, but what was the effect on their sales effort? Instead of pro-actively seeking out new customers they were reacting to the problems caused by failing to satisfy the existing customer base.

The thought that over 20 per cent of the work of a department is wasted does not sit easy with most managers, but unfortunately it is all too often true. Identifying and measuring it is the first step towards eliminating it. If we bury our heads in the sand and convince ourselves that we are the exception that proves the rule then the opportunity to improve is lost.

If the latent capacity is utilized and waste eliminated, the output of a week could be achieved in four days' work! We could all play golf one day a week and achieve the same objectives!

A boiled sweet factory thought it had no problems with quality. Any sweets that were damaged or not of the right shape were just put back in the cauldron and re-used. They thought that they had

no scrap, but 20 per cent of the output was being re-processed.

They were working seven days a week, three shifts a day and still could not meet demand. An expansion plan to increase the capacity by 15 per cent was being considered. During the planning of the new plant the industrial engineers became aware of the rework.

The shortage of capacity was caused by the poor control of the plant resulting in poor quality. Maintenance did not have time to clean the moulds as the plant was working flat out. Everyone just accepted the situation and carried on running to stand still.

The benefits that come from utilizing the latent capacity of a manufacturing plant are enormous. It allows for expansion without an increase in capital investment. It allows for increased output, without increasing the inputs. Improving the control optimizes the process and maximizes the return.

QUALITY, THE BEST ROUTE TO IMPROVING MORALE

The motivation of employees is a complex issue with many theories seeking to provide a level of understanding of the issues involved. It is generally accepted that people perform better when their work is recognized as being of a good standard and meeting the needs of the organization and the expectations of those around them – when they are seen by others to be providing quality.

Craftsmen have always been considered to take a pride in the items they produce and usually mark them so that they are immediately recognizable as their work. In the film industry all who have been associated with a film, from the boom man to the stars, have their names on the credits. They are proud of what they have done and want the world to know.

It is not just craftsmen and artists who take a pride in what they are doing. Everyone likes to see a job well done, and to know that their work is appreciated, by their customers and their colleagues. They like to meet needs and expectations – they like to provide quality.

In a cleaning company some of the staff were dissatisfied with the standards they were achieving. They wanted better chemicals, but the management would not provide them. Rather than be associated with an inferior standard they bought the materials they knew would work and provided quality for the customer. They took pride in their work as they felt they were being judged by their quality.

In an environment where quality is not being achieved there is a detrimental effect on the morale of the staff. Continual complaints concerning the quality of the service or products results in conflict and stress and a loss of self-esteem. This causes morale to fall and often performance suffers.

Where staff can see that the management's actions indicate that they do not put quality first, then that attitude spreads throughout the business.

In an engineering factory every product was fully tested against exacting specifications. The testers understood the importance of their work and were thorough with the tests.

When items failed to meet the specifications, and were required to meet production targets, the

management often over-ruled the testers and sent the products out.

After a while the testers realized that their work was not valued and was really of no significance in the operations of the company. Rather than see their decisions ignored they just stopped reporting the failures, and slowly the standards declined.

It was not until a new manager was appointed who refused to let failed items go out under any circumstances that the testers regained their self-respect and once again took pride in their work.

Building pride into people's work results in improved performance and improved quality. They know that when they produce quality, they are valued – valued by the customers and the management. Recognition of their performance promotes good quality and improves their attitude to work. They enjoy what they are doing, and this results in improved performance.

Many hotels and supermarkets have schemes where customers are asked to fill out questionnaires on the performance of the staff who have served them. These are then used to determine an 'employee of the week', who receives recognition from peers and is enrolled on a table of merit. This promotes quality and achieves improvements in standards and employee morale.

A company that has a reputation for quality generally has a workforce who are proud to be associated with their employer. They tell their friends with pride. The converse is also true. Where a company has a poor reputation for quality they keep quiet about where they work. Most people would prefer to say they worked for Marks and Spencer than for Joe's Discount Clothing!

Even if the reputation is not justified and they themselves feel they are doing a good job, their morale is affected by the reputation. To improve morale, you have to improve reputation, to improve reputation you have to improve quality.

Morale is not improved by bells and buzzers. It takes more than notices about quality to make improvements – in fact notices which do not align with actions can have a detrimental effect. If the vision or mission statement in reception does not ring true to the employees with the management's actions, then morale is damaged. If the computer screen flashes a 'Think Quality' message, and yet the employee feels the management does not 'act quality', then a cynical attitude results. That is bad for morale and bad for quality.

WE NEED QUALITY TO SURVIVE AND PROSPER

For businesses to survive and prosper they have to meet the needs and expectations of their customers and do so profitably. This means that they need to provide quality, and reduce the costs associated with a failure to provide quality.

Quality is not a luxury that can be addressed when there is time. It has to be the prime objective for all of the company, all the time, every time. Management has to believe in quality, be committed to it and be involved in making sure it happens. Without quality there can be no survival. With quality there is security, prosperity and growth.

3

WHO IS RESPONSIBLE FOR QUALITY?

SUMMARY

Quality is everybody's business and everyone is responsible for quality. These are basic truths which relate to all aspects of work. While it was once thought that it was feasible to have a separate class of employees called inspectors, who took responsibility for checking that things were right, it is now accepted that it is not possible to inspect quality into a product or service, it has to be built in by everyone involved.

Quality is a team game, and for success there needs to be a team plan. It is the management's job to develop the plan and ensure that it is communicated to and understood by everyone. The plan needs to ensure that everyone's objectives are aligned, and that all are working with the same aim.

If everyone is responsible for quality then it follows that everyone must have the authority to control quality. Without empowering employees with that authority it is pointless expecting them to be able to exercise the necessary control.

Management carries the overall responsibility for the whole organization. They need to set clear policies that are effectively communicated and they need to display their commitment to those policies – in actions as well as words.

Within the team each player has a role. They have to support the other players and meet their needs and expectations – they need to provide quality. This chain of quality goes right through the organization and like any chain it is only as strong as its weakest link.

RESPONSIBILITY FOR QUALITY STARTS AT THE TOP

It is true that the Chief Executive is responsible for everything in an organization. Quality is one aspect that has to receive special attention. Without quality the needs and expectations of the customers are jeopardized. Without quality profitability is compromised. Without quality reputation will be lost.

Quality has to start at the top, and for success it needs firm, clear leadership. There has to be a consistent approach to quality which is clearly defined and understood by all. This can only come from the top.

The executives of an organization have to take on board the responsibility for quality. To make it happen they need to define their policy, be committed to it and be involved in making it happen.

The responsibility for quality is balanced by the authority to make it happen. Ultimately it is the person at the top who has the authority to decide what happens. But on a day-to-day basis the authority to enact the detailed aspects of the policy is delegated.

The act of delegation is often misunderstood. A delegate has the authority to act on behalf of someone else. They are responsible for how they use that authority, but the person delegating the authority does not delegate the responsibility. They are still responsible. A new level of responsibility is created. The responsibility cannot be delegated.

Inherent in the act of delegation should be the establishing of policies, feedback and control. Without these, delegation becomes abdication. The amount of freedom within the policies varies and the degree and frequency of feedback required varies with the authority being delegated, but without clear policies and some feedback there is no delegation.

After a major disaster the chief executive said that

**he was not responsible, but he was going to make
sure it never happened again. He was responsible.**

**He was responsible for ensuring that systems
capable of preventing the disaster were in place,
and functioning efficiently. His acknowledge-
ment that he would ensure that it would not happen again recognizes this responsibility, a responsibility that cannot be delegated.**

In most businesses there are sophisticated systems in
place to control the spending and receiving of money.
Sometimes many approvals are required before money
is released or orders placed. The systems are audited and
control of the money is the highest priority.

To spend money great care is taken over the delegation
of the authority to act on behalf of the management.
This is after all the key measure of the success of the
company. Money is all about profit and loss and it needs
to be controlled.

Is the same level of control exercised over quality? Is the
same care taken to measure the rates of scrap and rework? Is the same level of feedback exercised over the
performance of the company in meeting the needs and
expectations of its customers?

**Concentrating on accounting systems, rather than
the processes producing the wealth of the
organization, is like a cricket team that loses a
match while deciding to improve the controls in
the method of recording the score. It is no use introducing a control to get five signatures before it
is recorded that a player has been bowled out. You
need to work on his batting ability so that he can
survive longer on the crease. To improve the performance you have to work with the players, not
the score-keepers.**

Just as management are responsible for ensuring the accounts of the company are under control, so they are responsible for the control of quality. They should ensure that they know the quality of performance just as well as the financial performance.

If the financial auditors reported that 20 per cent of the turnover was disappearing in fraud it would be addressed with the highest priority. If security discovered thefts of 20 per cent the police would be involved. Yet management often do not know what is lost through poor quality and it often exceeds 20 per cent.

Top management has to show all employees that they take quality seriously. For this to happen it is vital that communications are efficient, systems in place and seen to be operating and that management show that they place quality first. It is no good just talking about it, it is necessary to show that you mean it, are committed to it and are involved in achieving it. If you do not have the time to address quality, that sends a powerful message to everyone else.

Responsibility for quality starts at the top. For success to be achieved everyone needs to know and believe that quality comes first.

INSPECTORS CANNOT IMPROVE QUALITY

In the middle ages craftsmen were responsible for their own work. To practise their craft they were required to prove to their Guild that they were well trained and could practise their craft. They controlled their own quality.

With the Industrial Revolution came a new grade of worker. Depending on the industry, they were given titles such as checkers or inspectors and they did no work themselves, but just checked on the work of others. They pointed out the faults and others corrected them. They became responsible for making sure everything was right – they tried to achieve quality.

This practice still continues in some industries. On many building sites the 'clerk of works' is expected to produce a snagging list and the contractors correct the faults found. It is accepted practice, but is it good practice?

In a domestic refrigerator factory the accepted practice was for each fridge to be inspected by an inspector and a list of faults attached to the door. A rectifier came next and he spent his time correcting the listed faults. As each one was corrected, it was ticked off. The fridge was then re-inspected and each fault marked as cleared.

The inspector had no more eyes or knowledge than the rectifier and he certainly added no value. The roles were combined to inspector/rectifiers. They inspected and corrected as they went along. But more importantly they went back down the line to where the faults were being caused and spent time training to eliminate the faults.

The number of faults slowly went down and the quality improved. The people making the fridges became responsible for the quality of their operations. They became their own inspectors.

It makes more sense for everyone to inspect and test their own work and to be responsible for their own quality. That is how we operate in our personal lives. If we are putting up a shelf at home, or ironing a shirt, we check what we are doing as we go along. We make adjustments until we achieve the standard we want. We may refer to others for help or advice, or may receive unwanted comments, but at the end of the day we are responsible for the job.

The same must be true in our working lives. We must all be responsible for controlling the quality of our own work. Inspectors cannot inspect quality into a product or service. It is up to everyone to build quality in.

There is a tendency when you know an inspector is going to review your work not to take so much care. This equally applies to production operators and office workers. If you know someone is responsible for proofreading a letter or checking an invoice then you may take less care. If you know you are responsible for getting it right, and you accept that responsibility, you try to ensure it is right.

Having a separate team of inspectors is not only wasteful, it has been found to be highly inefficient. The process of inspection is well known to be fallible. Research has found that the percentage of faults found during inspection operations is often as low as 80 per cent. This has led to some organizations introducing double inspection in the hope that what one inspector misses another will find, but this only brings the result to around 95 per cent. It is not possible to achieve quality by inspection alone; quality can only be achieved by having processes that produce to the requirements.

QUALITY CHAINS – EVERYONE'S RESPONSIBILITY TO EACH OTHER

Recognizing that everyone is responsible for the quality of their own work is an important step towards achieving quality. To make it work it is necessary to define who does what. This changes a group of individuals into a team.

In an organization each individual can consider the relationships with those around in terms of supplier-customer links. Each person has others for whom they are completing tasks. These others can be considered as customers.

Sales representatives pass orders to the sales office, so the sales office are customers of the representatives and the representatives are suppliers to the office. The assembly shop passes finished machines to packing, so packing are customers of assembly and assembly are the suppliers of the packing department.

Viewing internal relationships in this manner allows everyone to have contact with their own customers. Everyone has customers they know, and those customers have needs and expectations. To achieve quality it is necessary to determine and understand those needs and expectations and to seek to develop and meet them.

By providing quality for our internal customers we increase the probability that quality will be provided for the external customers. But we also increase the efficiency of the business, reduce friction between colleagues and align objectives through the business.

Viewed in this way quality can be seen as a chain running right through the business, with each person as a link in the chain. The chain needs to run smoothly for the business to run smoothly, and where there is friction or stress between links it is necessary to improve quality at the interface.

Each link needs to know and understand the needs of the adjacent links and to be responsive to those needs. By meeting these needs the objectives of the whole organization are achieved.

Considering the organization as a series of links enables individuals to understand their own responsibility for quality. Even when employees have no direct contact with the customer, and their work seems obscure, by considering their internal customers they can see the value of their contribution.

In many situations the 'product' being supplied through the chain is information. This supply of information is vital to the achievement of quality. Communication, the supply of information, creates some interesting responsibilities when analysed through supplier-customer chains.

As with all customer-supplier links, it is the responsibility of the supplier to meet the needs and expectations of the customer. A good supplier does not assume those needs, but sets about discovering and understanding what they are.

In a business we do not just supply each other with products, indeed many people never see the products the business supplies. They only handle information. Their work is about communication and the customer-supplier link is vital for communication to be efficient.

Considering communication clearly illustrates the responsibility of the supplier to consider the customer, the sender of the information to consider the receiver. As many communications flow from management to the staff, it follows that the management, with respect to the information provided, are the suppliers to their staff. The staff are the customers, and for quality to be achieved the information must be in a form that is understandable to them.

Management should determine the needs of their staff with respect to information, its detail, timing and presentation, and meet those needs. They are responsible for providing quality communications. This responsibility for quality information covers the whole range of management communication, from the simple informal request to formal procedures and memos. In every case the communication must be appropriate to the receiver and understood by them.

The most brilliant plan which is poorly communicated is not likely to succeed. Communication is essential to success.

RESPONSIBILITY FOR QUALITY IN SALES

The chain of quality starts with sales and marketing. They have the responsibility to ensure that the customers' needs are accurately identified and defined. With bespoke products or services this may revolve around discussions with the potential customers to establish needs. With products and services of a more standard nature, market research plays a vital part in establishing those needs.

In establishing the needs of the customer the approach of finding the minimum specification that will be acceptable is clearly not a quality approach. The specification must meet the current needs, consider the customers' present expectations and endeavour to anticipate future expectations.

Among the needs and expectations there has to be a consideration of the price the customer is prepared to pay. Where there are different grades of specification, perhaps with different levels of accessories or luxury, achieving quality does not imply delivering the highest specification. It is, rather, the establishment of the correct specification for the customer, taking account of the price to be paid.

A recently widowed middle-aged lady went into a car showroom. She had received life insurance following her husband's death and wanted to buy a

new car. Price was not really a factor when she discussed the choice with the salesman.

The car he would have bought in her position was a sporty model at the top of the range. He showed her this car and took her for a ride in it. She was impressed and he convinced her it was the right car for her. She agreed to buy it and took down the details of the model to fix the insurance.

Her insurance broker was more professional and pointed out the disadvantages of the vehicle – the higher insurance costs, the propensity for sporty models to be stolen by joy riders and the higher running costs. He was looking at the purchase from her point of view.

The sale was duly cancelled and she went elsewhere. She no longer trusted the salesman to provide her with good advice.

Sales have to determine what is best for the customer and offer the best product or service available. It is better to admit that you have nothing suitable than to take on a contract that results in a dissatisfied customer.

Determining market needs is an important prerequisite to the provision of quality. This has to be done systematically and objectively to ensure that plans based on the information are realistic and achievable. Knowledge of relevant legislation and expected performance and reliability are vital for quality to be provided, and sales and marketing have the responsibility for their determination.

Sales have to ensure that all the information provided to the customer is accurate and cannot be misinterpreted. This is a fundamental principle of good quality. Small print, intended to allow you to hide your responsibilities, does not lead to quality and is incompatible with good customer relations.

Ensuring clear and concise communications with customers is fundamental to quality and viable customer relationships. Vague specifications and poor definitions inevitably lead to misunderstandings and dissatisfaction.

Sales have a clear responsibility to ensure that all aspects of the customer interface are clearly defined and that the capability exists to meet the contract. This can only be achieved by communications focused on the customer that honestly describe the expected outcomes from the contract.

Even in the best run business there are times when the customer decides to complain. While these complaints do indicate a level of dissatisfaction, it is better to encourage complaints than never to find out what your customers think.

Complaints answered tactfully and effectively do not have to result in a loss of customers, and indeed a positive response can enhance relationships. They also provide opportunities to learn about the business and to improve quality.

Sales are responsible for actions needed to compensate customers for poor quality, but this should not be seen as the end of the responsibility. They need to ensure that the customers' complaints are investigated objectively and that the causes are addressed. Communication of these actions back to the customer builds the relationship and confidence in the future and can change a problem into an opportunity.

RESPONSIBILITY FOR QUALITY IN DESIGN
The design function provides the vital link between the ideas developed in sales and the fulfilment provided by

operations. Whether it is a totally new product or an enhancement in service level, for success it is necessary for quality to be a high priority during the design process.

While designers know they have the responsibility to ensure that their designs provide quality for external customers, it is just as important to ensure that quality is provided for internal customers. They have needs and expectations and it is vital that they are considered by the design process.

The design process starts with a clear specification of the requirements, and generally the design function is responsible for ensuring that this is comprehensive and covers all legal requirements. It needs to be in a form that can be clearly understood by non-technical personnel in other functions and, where the design is for identified customers, by those customers.

As the design progresses there is a responsibility for ensuring that there are meaningful reviews by the other functions – the internal customers. For efficient results they need to be part of the team that develops and agrees the design.

The design of the chassis for a new range of trucks failed to take account of the method of assembly to be used. The designers placed bolts so close to other parts on the chassis that it was not possible for the fitters to get a spanner on to the heads to tighten them with power tools. The designers had totally failed to provide a quality design for the assembly line!

Design is generally where the product and service expertise lies in a business. This expertise needs to be used to prepare communications which clearly define the requirements. When this is not done there are communication problems which lead to problems with quality. It is the responsibility of design to establish the standards and to ensure that these are clearly defined so that everyone understands what is to be delivered.

A clear specification is important to both the internal and external customers. Without it important issues are open to interpretation, and inevitably misinterpretation. The design team has the responsibility of ensuring that the features and characteristics of the product or service are unambiguously defined, and defined so that they can be understood by the customers, both internal and external.

Design is vital for quality to be achieved. Without a design that totally meets customer requirements there is no chance for the rest of the business to deliver quality. This is the responsibility the design function has for quality.

RESPONSIBILITY IN PURCHASING
Many businesses rely on others to supply parts or services which form an integral part of their core business. This reliance links suppliers and sub-contractors into the quality chain. Their performance is often critical to the achievement of quality and this performance is the responsibility of purchasing.

Purchasing have the responsibility for the communications between the business and its suppliers. They have to ensure that the requirements are clearly defined and understood. Without this, quality cannot be achieved.

As well as communicating the requirements efficiently purchasing also have the responsibility for selecting suppliers who are capable of delivering those requirements.

The long-term achievement of quality can only be

achieved by building long-term relationships with suppliers. Their role in the quality chain needs to be respected and contracts built on loyalty and trust are better than continual bargaining to find the cheapest short-term cost.

Purchasing are responsible for building these relationships and for working with suppliers to improve quality. This responsibility, in businesses that have a large purchased content to their work, makes the purchasing function vital to the achievement of quality.

RESPONSIBILITY FOR QUALITY IN OPERATIONS

The operations function in a business is responsible for the delivery of the service or the production of the products. Its name varies, depending on the nature of the business, but in essence its responsibility for quality is the same.

Operations are responsible for ensuring the quality of the product or service. This responsibility requires them to control the processes that achieve quality. Control requires the assessment of the output of a process to determine any changes required to the inputs to that process. This is the responsibility of the operations function.

Assessment of the output of a process, without using the information for control, will not achieve quality. It may enable occurrences of poor quality to be detected and steps taken to prevent them reaching the customer, but quality cannot be achieved through inspection and testing alone.

Operations are responsible for determining the capability of their processes and for ensuring their compatibility with the requirements. If the processes are not capable, then quality cannot be consistently achieved. If the processes are capable then they require control to ensure quality.

Operations management have the responsibility for establishing and communicating clear standards against which performance can be assessed. Without such standards there can be no control. Without control there can be no quality.

The assessment of performance requires a measuring system appropriate to the standard. This may require complex equipment to determine the size or finish of products, or a simple record of the time the customer has to wait. Without the assessment of performance, the achievement of the standard is an unknown, so the achievement of quality is an unknown.

The establishment of standards and assessment are pre-requisites for control. In themselves they do not establish control. For control to exist, actions need to be taken based on the assessment to bring the performance back to standard. These actions may be simple or complex depending on the level in the organization, but the operations management have the responsibility for ensuring they occur and are effective.

RESPONSIBILITY FOR QUALITY IN PERSONNEL

The employees of a business are its major asset. They might not show on the balance sheet, but without them there is no business. It is through them that the business achieves its objectives, and their training and motivation are essential to a successful business.

The personnel function is generally not directly responsible for the work of the employees, but their actions can have a direct effect on them. If the general atmosphere is employee-focused then quality is more likely to result. If the atmosphere is one of fear and coercion then it is unlikely that quality will be achieved.

Quality requires a trained workforce, and the assessment and meeting of their training needs is vital for success. Personnel is responsible for implementing and delivering a positive training policy that aims to develop the employees for the operation and growth of the business. This development has to address not only the technical skills required, but also wider issues of problem solving, motivation and organization.

Quality requires a team approach by the whole workforce with aligned objectives. Personnel have a role in achieving this through the development of management and employees.

RESPONSIBILITY FOR QUALITY IN FINANCE

The role of finance in a business is generally two-fold. Firstly to control the flow of money within the business and secondly to report on where costs are incurred. On the face of it these two functions have little to do with the achievement of quality.

The payment of suppliers and sub-contractors can have a serious effect on their attitude to a business and their willingness to provide a quality service. Given the choice between dealing with an urgent request from a good payer and one from a poor payer, most businesses opt for the good payer. From this it follows that finance can have a direct effect on quality.

In many businesses it is estimated that the non-achievement of quality costs at least 20 per cent of turnover. Rework, scrap and warranty are all costs which are avoidable if the performance is right first time.

Unfortunately these costs are usually well hidden in the system or accepted as part of the normal business operation. Finance have a responsibility to provide management with costing information and this should extend to the measurement of the cost of quality. Once these figures are known then the savings that can be achieved become apparent. Once the savings become apparent then the justification of corrective actions becomes easier.

The achievement of quality is a team game and finance have a responsibility for ensuring the team know how they are performing in financial terms. After all, finance is the life blood of the business and unless the various flows are measured there is a danger that the continual bleeding caused by poor quality will eventually lead to a non-viable condition.

OVERALL MANAGEMENT RESPONSIBILITY

Whilst each function in a business has clear responsibilities for quality it must not be forgotten that quality is a team game. Management have the overall responsibility to ensure that departmental and sectional objectives and rivalries are suppressed to ensure customer satisfaction, to ensure quality.

When concerns are identified with quality it is vital that management do not allow 'witch hunts' to start with one department blaming another and each defending their own interests. Quality is not about blame. Quality is about treating each shortfall of performance as an opportunity to improve, to improve methods, materials, communications and people. This can only be truly achieved if everyone has aligned objectives and shares the responsibility for working to get it right.

Managers have to ensure that they work well together, and that their staff work well together. This will not be achieved if their actions and words indicate they have no respect for others. Off-the-cuff criticisms of the performance of other sections can all too easily be taken out of context and lead to the situation where there is no respect for each other's work.

Above all management must adopt the correct attitude to quality at all times. They must lead by example and show everyone that they believe it is essential to make customer satisfaction the highest priority, to ensure that customers always get value from the business and so value the business. They have to ensure quality.

HOW IS QUALITY ACHIEVED?

SUMMARY

Some organizations exceed their customers' wishes without it being an issue. Quality is a natural result of their work, it just happens. But even these fortunate organizations need to be aware of how their processes perform if they are going to maintain quality.

What is considered quality today, may be unacceptable tomorrow. Consistent achievement of quality requires a clear policy which involves the whole business and has full commitment from the top.

The implementation of this policy must be the priority of everyone. This requires an understanding and control of the operational processes of the business. It is these processes that discover what the customers really want, define products or services to provide value and ensure that these are delivered day in, day out.

These processes are integrated into a system which assures quality. This system starts in sales and marketing and ends with a delighted customer. Everything between these two points needs to be controlled for quality to be achieved.

Inherent in control are three steps: the measurement of performance; a comparison with a standard; and actions to bring the performance back to the standard or to improve the standard.

Control is best achieved at a local level, with the people operating the process being empowered to control it. Empowerment leads to the development of teamwork and the harnessing of the human resource of the whole organization, but requires good communications and often a transformation of the thinking of the management. Management need to value their employees, train them to the limit of their potential, break down any departmental barriers and lead them, through example, to develop and deliver products and services which delight their customers.

A CLEAR COMMITMENT

A clear management commitment to quality has to be the starting point of any quality programme. Nothing is ever achieved without commitment, and since quality is the responsibility of the whole business, that commitment must be from the top. The most senior management need to understand the issues relating to quality and be committed to ensure that quality is a priority. Without real commitment quality will not be continuously achieved.

Putting this commitment into action requires its communication to all – employees, customers and suppliers. Some form of quality policy, vision, mission statement or a series of quality objectives is the common starting point of this communication. These announcements have slight differences, but a common purpose – to define and clarify the position on quality.

Organizations arrive at fine words saying where they stand and what they believe. These words should be the result of a management process, a process that can be as important as the result. For many management teams it is the first time they spend time discussing the meaning of quality in their business and decide where they stand. The outcome may be a fine statement, but it should be their own words in which they believe, not those borrowed from another source. Establishing the words has value – and many businesses find it a significant step along the road to total quality.

The board of a furniture manufacturer was required to write a quality policy for its ISO 9000

registration. For the first time, the members sat down together and discussed what quality meant to them and their business. Previously they had discussed sales, marketing, finance, product development and production, but never quality.

Out of the discussion came a policy they were all happy to sign and publish, but more importantly the discussion had focused their minds on quality. They all had a better understanding of what they were trying to achieve.

Establishing the intentions of the business is only the starting point of quality. For these to be achieved resources have to be allocated. It is no good stating what the business intends to do and then not providing the time or money to ensure it happens. This is just as much a part of commitment as the generation of fine words.

The preparation and publication of a policy, vision or mission statement for quality commit the management to quality. It becomes their target, but if they waver in following it then it makes them the target. They have to 'walk the talk'. A published statement cannot be just an empty collection of words, it has to represent a firm commitment, backed up by plans, resources and actions.

Customer expectations continually change. The achievement of quality requires the vision and direction to look at these changes and anticipate them. What is considered excellent today becomes mediocre or worthless tomorrow. The commitment to quality should be to embrace this requirement for continual improvement. To set the pace there needs to be a proactive drive for improvement – of product specifications, service standards and staff performance. All these are essential to achieve quality.

A SYSTEM TO MAKE IT HAPPEN

Commitments, visions, mission statements and policies are all essential if quality is to be achieved, but they are not enough. Without a system to make it happen, they are just empty words. A system is required to deliver quality and that system is the 'quality system'.

All businesses have a quality system, but often it is not recognized as such. A quality system is composed of the processes by which a business identifies, defines and meets its customers' changing needs and expectations – it is the game plan of the business.

Even a golf club has a quality system. It comprises the processes used to select new members, allocate lockers, regulate starting times, cut the grass and regulate the bars. All of these processes are essential for the members to enjoy their golf. All of these processes, and many more, are part of the quality system.

Each business is unique. It may have similar general objectives as others, but it achieves these in different ways. These differences arise from within the business and its environment – the resources it has, the service it provides, the market in which it operates and the staff who work in it. From this it follows that the quality system of a business needs to be unique, if it is to efficiently meet the objectives of the business.

Within the quality system are all the operational processes which are used to provide quality. These processes may start with sales and marketing and then go right through to delivery and installation. They are the processes by which the business makes it happen – and unless these processes provide quality then the business is doomed to failure.

The operational processes are supported by organizational processes. These typically include the personnel, finance and other administrative functions which are essential for the mainstream processes to function efficiently. While not directly providing quality to the external customers, these functions are needed by the internal customers and are essential for a viable business.

Quality starts with the first contact with a potential customer, but from that point onwards it never ends. As long as there is a memory of the service, or even better a product performing reliably, then quality still exists. A truly delighted customer is the best advertisement for the next sale.

The first contact is vital as you have only one chance to make a first impression. This impression may be the only impression, so get it right.

A good first contact with a customer is only that. For quality to be achieved all the processes used by the business need to be understood and controlled. It is these processes that provide quality. It is these processes that have to be quality processes.

In most businesses some processes involve many departments and cross functional boundaries. For efficient control these boundaries must be subjugated to the efficiency of the processes. Functional or sectional rivalries do not produce quality. Departments working with shared, aligned objectives produce a team targeted at the customer, at quality.

If the process of planning involves sales, design, purchasing, engineering, finance and production, then the objectives of that process should take priority over the objectives of each of the contributing departments. The departments' aims are only part of the business aim of pleasing the customer; the overriding aim has to be to achieve quality, as without quality there will be no business.

If quality is achieved through the quality system, it follows that to improve quality we need to change that system.

Before making changes it is essential that we understand the present. This is the starting point for improving performance; this is the starting point for improving quality.

DEFINING YOUR PROCESSES

The quality system is composed of a series of interrelated processes – each process a link in the quality system chain. Each process has to achieve objectives, and the meeting of these should assure quality. Failure to meet one objective, causes the whole system to fail.

To understand the quality system you need to start by identifying each process, to break down the whole system into individual processes; to define the individual links in the quality chain.

Each process has objectives. It takes inputs and achieves outputs from them. Many processes operate within a single department, or are even done by one person. Where more are involved let each process include all of the activities, and all the inputs involved in meeting the objectives. Do not be constrained by departmental boundaries.

The identification of the processes should be in terms which are meaningful to your business. If you talk about 'order entry', use those words as the process title. Select process titles that are meaningful to you. This encourages ownership of the processes by the staff who use them.

Once identified the processes can be analysed and described. This may sound like a complex operation, but it usually just involves sitting with the people who operate the process and recording the details of what is done. This is the starting point, and even taking this step may identify opportunities to standardize and improve.

It is amazing how often it is found that people doing the same job in the same business develop different methods. This is not a problem, but understanding why can lead to the development of a standard process or method, which is more efficient.

When an analysis of the invoicing system of one company was done, it was found that five separate processes were used. The original dual entries in a ledger had been replaced long ago and now, after four improvements, the system was fully computerized. As each new system was made, the old one was kept in case of teething problems. No one had stopped the old processes being used!

The analysis and recording of the process bring differences out and stimulate discussion and agreement on the optimum process. Implementing the optimum process ensures a uniformity of approach and prevents confusion when staff cover for each other.

To efficiently control the various processes in a business it is essential that the inputs to those processes are known. The output from any process is only influenced by the inputs, and the inputs need to be controlled to control the output.

Inputs to processes may be in the form of machines, materials, methods, people and the whole environment in which the process operates. Each of these inputs influences the performance of the process to a greater or lesser extent. Any of these inputs may influence quality.

Fig. 4.1

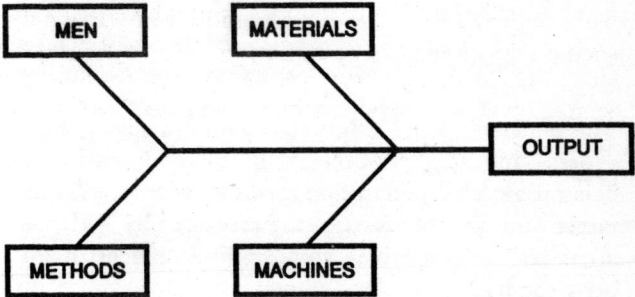

Fishbone diagram

To control a process it is necessary to understand it – what it should achieve and who does what, when and how.

Describing a process ensures that everyone associated with it understands what is to be done. The description is a communication to staff to indicate what is needed. It provides a standard method for training and control.

Like all communications the description needs to be aimed at the receiver, the reader and user of the description. The form of the description needs to be selected for those users and must be appropriate for their use. This may be achieved by a simple procedure, or for technical processes a flow chart may be more appropriate. Whatever form is chosen it must be understandable to the users.

The level of detail in the procedure should take account of the training and experience of those who will read it.

There is no need to tell a driver how to start a car or a computer operator how to use a keyboard. These are basic skills which are required by those who carry out such processes and can be assumed in the procedure.

This understanding needs to start with an analysis of the process and a description of the methods currently being used. This description forms the basis for future improvements. Analysis of the processes by itself, to arrive at the description, often reveals potential improvements.

In processes that involve many people it is common to find that there are differences in the way in which they work. There may be no overall picture of the process and individuals may just concentrate on their own part without seeing the whole. The procedures describe the processes and their preparation allows for agreement on the process and acceptance of the method to be used.

Their use does not end there. Good procedures that are readily available become vital reference documents, particularly for processes that occur infrequently. They allow everyone to know what should be done and provide a base for control.

The present methods are the starting points as they relate to current performance. If improvement is required, then change is needed. Unless you know what you are currently doing change can be impossible. Unless the present is understood change can bring disruption.

Procedures should not be carved in stone. As the business needs change then they should change. They are an ideal way to implement and control change as they provide a clear communication of what is required. They should become a living part of the structure of the business, the natural place for all to turn to know how quality should be achieved.

AUDITING THE SYSTEM

The procedures indicate what should be done, but to ensure their accuracy, and to confirm their implementation, it is beneficial to audit the procedures. While this may sound like an over-bureaucratic process, when approached constructively it provides an ideal way to look for opportunities to improve.

An audit is the opportunity to ask those involved in a process to show how they work and to compare it with the written description, procedure or flow chart. The audit identifies whether the description is inaccurate or the implementation incomplete. Either condition provides an opportunity to improve by either changing the description or retraining the staff concerned.

Auditing the whole quality system provides a proactive route for continual improvement. It allows for the processes of the business to be reviewed on a routine basis and gives confirmation that the quality system is meeting current needs. It provides evidence that the business is committed to quality and is a useful management technique for proving the adequacy of the system.

A car is composed of several systems. These include braking, steering, power and transmission. A prudent driver does not wait for things to go wrong but has the systems checked on a frequent basis to *find* any problems before they *cause* problems. Even the imprudent are obliged to have the minimum standards checked on older cars through the MOT testing system.

During audits it is important to explain that it is the

system that is being audited, not the people. While the people are the carriers of the system, the audit is not to try to catch them out, but to show that the system is operating as planned. Its object is to find ways to improve the procedures, operations and processes, and hence to improve quality.

Audits identify opportunities to improve, and to get any benefit from the audit these opportunities need to be taken. This leads to corrective and preventative actions, actions that address the root causes of any concerns identified and seek to eliminate them. Subsequent audits can confirm the efficiency of corrective actions.

FINDING THE 'VOICE' OF YOUR PROCESSES

Having described the processes of the business you know how they operate and what each of them is intended to achieve. The audits will have ensured that things are operating in line with the procedures and there should be some level of stability and control.

If quality is being achieved then it is tempting to think everything is fine. You have committed the company to quality, defined how you want the business to work and checked that it is operating according to your plans. You are meeting your customers' requirements and achieving quality, so you are a quality business.

That is a good start, but to leave it there is like deciding to sail to New York, setting the course and checking that you are still on the same setting. You need a method of checking your performance; you need to know the 'voice' of your processes.

When you measure the output of any process, it is found to vary. The variations may be small, and may be acceptable to you and your customers, but they still need to be known and understood.

The collection of information about the performance of a process is the next step on the quality road. Data may be simple measurements of the size of a feature of a product produced by a process, the time taken to process an order or the volume of sales shipped in a month. These figures give information on the performance of the processes to which they relate, but to be of value they need to be viewed within their own context.

Fig. 4.2

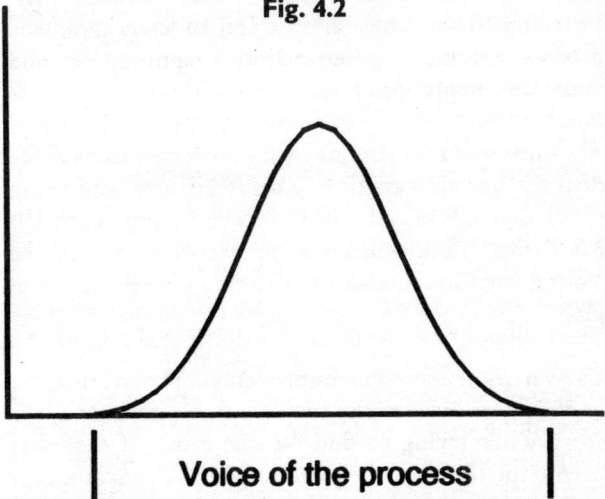

Voice of the process

These figures enable you to hear the process, but to be able to listen to the process you need to analyse the figures. Analysis removes noise made by the process and enables you to find the voice of the process.

The voice of the process is independent of the specifications. These are the voice of the customer – what the customer, either internal or external, wants. The voice of the customer does not affect the voice of the process, only inputs to the process can affect the voice of the process.

The interpretation of data requires a good understanding of statistics and their application to business. This is a subject in its own right and is beyond the scope of this book, but it is necessary to accept a key premise on which statistical process control is based if quality is to be achieved.

This premise, which can be shown to be true, indicates that there is a natural variation in any process when it is in control. This variation is an inherent part of the output of the process. This is the voice of the process. Listening to this voice allows you to learn about the process and know when action is appropriate, and when it is inappropriate.

The output of a process may vary on occasions by more than the natural variation. This is because something has changed. It may not be immediately apparent what has changed, but whenever the variation exceeds the natural variation it is safe to assume a change has taken place.

The variation may show improvement in performance, or it may show deterioration, and in either case it is worthwhile trying to find out the cause. If there has been improvement, then you will wish to encourage it to happen again. If there has been deterioration then you will wish to prevent it happening again. In both cases you need to know why.

Unless you understand the nature of the variation of a process there is a danger that you will interfere with the natural performance. You cannot control a process unless you know its natural variation. Any attempt to do so is likely to increase the degree of variation, not reduce it.

In a factory producing rubber mouldings the operator controlled the extrusion machine by weighing a billet every now and then. If the billet

was heavier or lighter than the target, he adjusted the machine.

When the variation in weight from the machine was analysed it was found that there was less variation when no adjustments were made. The operator, by using a sample of one weight to determine the need for adjustment, was increasing the variation.

The weighing method was changed so that batches of five billets were taken and the weight of the five used to detect the need to adjust. Fewer adjustments were made and the output had less variation.

If the voice of the process is within the voice of the customer, then the process is capable of meeting customers' requirements. Control is still needed to ensure that the process is set correctly and to identify any changes, but with control the customers' requirements will be achieved. Quality will be achieved.

Fig. 4.3

Voice of the customer
Specification

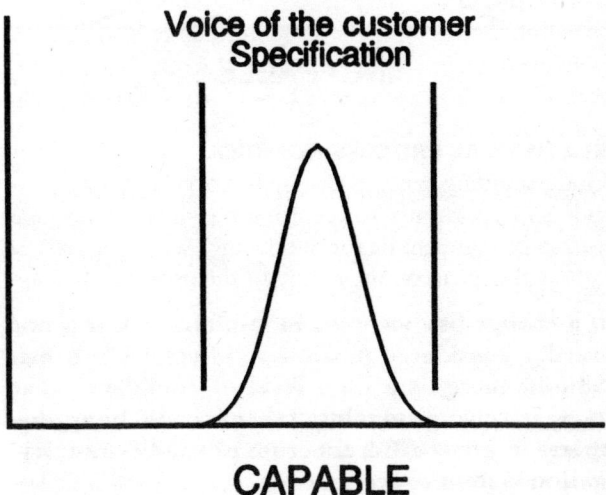

CAPABLE

If the voice of the process is greater than the voice of the customer then no control can assure consistent quality. The best that can be achieved is to minimize the occasions on which the requirements are not achieved by carefully setting the process and watching for changes. For consistent quality the process needs to be improved to reduce the variation, or the customers' requirements need to be reviewed to establish compatibility.

Fig. 4.4

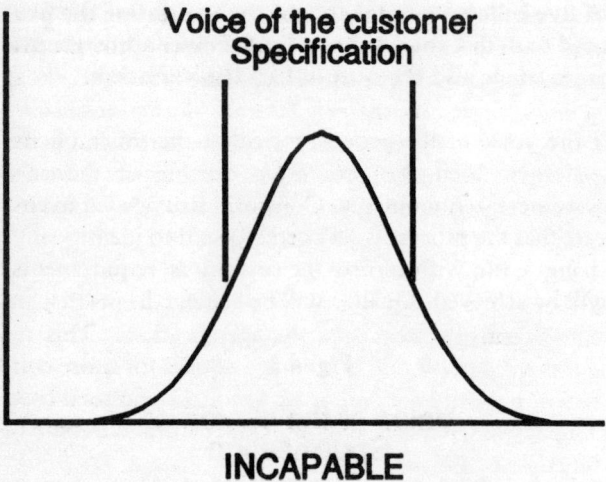

Voice of the customer
Specification

INCAPABLE

STATISTICAL PROCESS CONTROL
Understanding when a change has occurred may provide an opportunity to control the process, or to take actions to compensate for the change. Which of these is true will depend on the nature of the process.

If a change has occurred in rainfall, then it is not usually considered possible to affect the process. Should there be a high level of confidence that there is a change in rainfall then it could be appropriate to grow different crops or modify the irrigation system to compensate.

The use of statistical techniques is valuable for determining when it is appropriate to take action, and just as importantly when action should not be taken. The statistics are a tool to identify the need for action, but control is achieved through the actions not through the statistics. Unless the techniques are used to provide information while the process is in progress, and so allow actions to be taken immediately, we have statistical process monitoring, not control.

For control to be achieved the staff operating the process need to know what actions will bring the process under control. They need authority to take those actions, or to stop the process until the actions can be taken. This is the essence of process control and is the route you must take to ensure that the outputs from the processes meet the specifications, that they provide quality.

Often processes can be controlled within limits that are significantly 'better' than the specifications. This reduces the variation in output and allows for more consistent performance and often a reduction in total cost. This continual improvement is the natural outcome of improved control.

A conflict may arise when a variation is detected which indicates that control is appropriate, yet when output is still acceptable to the customer. Do you take action to keep the variation to the minimum, or take no action and let the process vary excessively – though still within specifications? There is no easy answer, but if quality is really about value for the customer, then the cost of any action taken should be less than the value added.

The customer may be accepting the variation, not because it is something he wants, but because it is something he has to accept. Another supplier may improve control and reduce the variation. This could give the other supplier an advantage. You must never accept that the customers' requirements are fixed. Customers have continually changing expectations. If you do not control your variations then the customer may find someone who will.

PROCESS IMPROVEMENT

Quality can only be achieved by controlling the processes of the business. It is processes that produce the output; it is processes that produce quality.

Inspecting the output after processing is complete may identify a failure to produce quality, but it cannot affect the process. The process is only affected by its inputs, and to achieve quality these need to be understood and controlled.

If a process is not achieving quality, or is not in control, then change is required. The change must be made to the inputs to the process, there is no other way to achieve change.

Knowledge of what actions can achieve improved control may not be immediately available. This should not mean that excessive variation is accepted, but that there is an opportunity to improve.

A detailed study of the process has to start from the premise that a change to the output can only be caused by a change to an input. Where this relationship is not apparent, it is because a lack of understanding of the performance of the process. That can only be remedied by learning more about the process. It is through learning about a process that it changes from a 'black art' to a technology.

Learning more about processes, their inputs and how

variations are caused, is vital if they are to be improved. This learning is not a one-off affair, but a continual cycle of Plan, Do, Study and Act – the PDSA cycle.

Fig. 4.5

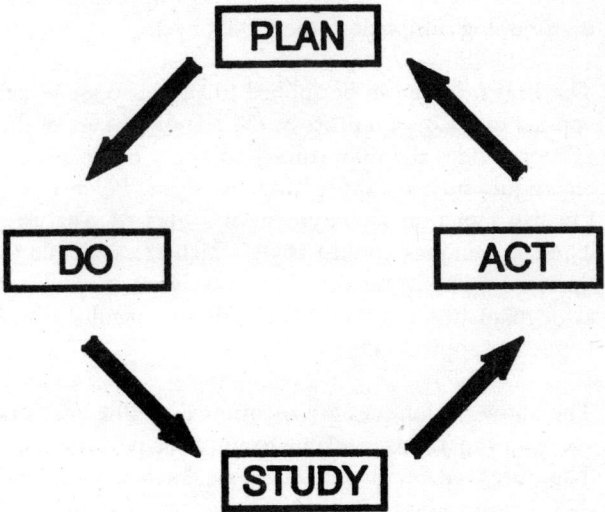

PDSA cycle

This cycle has been adopted by the traditional total quality movement to describe the scientific approach to process improvement. It illustrates the need to ensure that 'seat of the pants' management is replaced by a systematic approach which starts with a plan. This plan is then carried out, maybe initially as a pilot exercise. The effect of the plan on the performance of the process is then studied and corrective actions developed. The plan may then be implemented across the board. These actions form part of a plan and the cycle is repeated.

In the study phase of the cycle there are numerous techniques that can be used. Data collection, Pareto Analysis, Cause and Effect Diagrams, Selection Analysis and Brainstorming are all techniques conventionally associated with process improvement. These techniques, and many others, are tools to assist the discovery of the optimum methods. They are not as important as the methodology implicit in the PDSA cycle.

The PDSA cycle can be applied to any process. When applied to the design process, the planning stage of the cycle provides the opportunity to apply other quality techniques such as Failure Mode Analysis, Poka-Yoke, Quality Function Deployment and Hazard Analysis. These techniques are just tools which are available to those who pursue quality. In themselves they will not achieve quality, but their use should be considered and applied as appropriate.

The above techniques are mentioned to illustrate the variety of methods available to improve performance. These are well documented in more detailed books and their application can be beneficial in many businesses. They should be studied and used as the need arises.

QUALITY CIRCLES

Quality Circles, Quality Improvement Groups and Process Improvement Groups are examples of the titles given in different organizations to groups of employees who work together on improving the processes they use. The objective of the groups is to improve the quality of the performance of the processes.

Quality Circles operate widely throughout Japan and are common in some industries in the USA and UK. Different circles have developed different ways of operating and there are varying ground rules, but common across all successful groups are some key factors.

The members of the groups are all trained in a range of problem-solving and statistical analysis techniques. These are then used by the groups to systematically study the processes directly associated with the members of the group. Outside expertise is used as necessary, but the groups operate with a fair degree of autonomy.

The groups study problems, often of their own choosing, which they believe will lead to improvements in quality. Their findings are developed by the group into proposals for their line management. If accepted, they are implemented. The effects of the changes made are studied by the group in line with the PDSA cycle.

These groups enable their members to contribute to the quality of their processes. They harness the human resources of the business to improve its performance. They allow the employees to develop their skills and potential to the limit of their abilities and interests.

A quality circle in an engine factory decided to look at the manufacture of a critical part. It was a long-standing problem that the management had been trying to solve for years.

Working as a team, and involving the tool room and process engineering, they developed a new method of machining that improved the capability of the process. Within three months they had reduced a scrap rate of 30 per cent to less than one per cent! Their intimate knowledge of the processes gave them advantages over the management team.

Quality Circles have been successful where the management has given them full support and recognition. Empowering the circles to question their processes increases the commitment of the members to continual improvement. It recognizes the role of all in the quality chain to improve the performance of that chain. It changes process operators into process controllers.

Quality Circles have not succeeded where they have been introduced without adequate training, management commitment and real empowerment. If they are not allowed to truly contribute to the function of their processes then the members see them as a cynical management attempt to get something for nothing.

Commitment to Quality Circles requires a change in the thinking of many management teams. They have to recognize that they do not have all the answers. Operators, both in offices and factories, have much to contribute to their methods of working. They are the people who use the processes day in and day out; they might lack technical knowledge, but their contribution can lead to improvements.

Circles prosper best in times of expansion. The improvements in performance may then lead to redeployment, but not unemployment. In times of crisis it requires real commitment to develop methods of improving performance and possibly reducing the workforce. This does not rule out their use in these circumstances, but greater leadership is required than in the good times.

QUALITY COSTS
The determination of the cost of quality in a business is seen by many as an important part of achieving quality. It provides a focus for management and information to justify the commitment to quality.

Quality costs are conventionally divided into three separate areas. These are failure costs, appraisal costs and prevention costs. Together they make the total cost of quality in a business.

Failure costs result from the failure of the business to achieve a performance that delivers quality first time. They are the costs related to reject items, late deliveries, retyped reports, customer complaints and warranty. These costs are avoidable if the processes perform as required.

Appraisal costs arise directly out of activities intended to detect whether quality has been achieved. They are the costs resulting from inspection, test, review, checking draft documents and proofreading. These activities are considered to add nothing to the process; they are necessary to confirm the process has worked efficiently. Appraisal activities identify the failures.

Prevention costs arise from actions taken by the business to ensure that failures do not arise. They are the costs associated with planning, training, process improvement and many other management activities that seek to prevent failure, that seek to improve quality.

Conventionally it is found that when these costs are measured in a business the failure costs may be as high as 20 per cent of sales turnover, the appraisal costs as high as five per cent, but the prevention costs less than one per cent. It is argued that an increase in prevention activities should reduce the need for appraisal and reduce the incidence of failure.

This argument is self-evident, but having figures to show the potential savings has been found to make it more persuasive. However, as with all figures, once produced, they are often questioned, and disputes about the actual values can detract from the validity of the argument.

The difference between appraisal and prevention activities can be almost artificial. A police radar trap appraises the speed of cars to check when they are outside the permissible limit. It is there to find failures and is an appraisal cost. Because we know of the existence of such traps our driving is modified. It is therefore also a prevention cost.

In reality all a business is really interested in is the size of its failure cost. This alone should provide a justification and incentive to improve the processes.

Failure costs may be equally difficult to measure. Scrap, rework and rejects are all easy to determine in theory. If the working environment is not an open one, one in which improvements are sought, many of these costs can be hidden.

The costs associated with the loss of a customer because of a poor performance are even more difficult to detect. To regain that customer, or to find others to replace him, is really a failure cost.

Knowledge of the quality costs of a business is clearly useful in the drive to achieve quality. Such costs provide an incentive, a justification for action and a measure of progress. They help focus management on quality and provide a reason for commitment to quality.

The measurement of quality costs is part of the achievement of quality. It is not a vital part, and the accuracy of the exercise should be limited. If you know the failure costs are 20 per cent of turnover, the decision is the same as if they were 15 per cent or 25 per cent – you still need to do something to reduce them!

MANAGING FOR QUALITY

Managing for quality starts with commitment, but it never ends. For quality to be achieved the commitment must be embodied in an all-out drive to give quality the highest priority. In all decisions, quality should be considered.

Quality is an integral part of the business. Quality is not an 'add on' or an 'optional extra'. Quality is not something that can be considered in isolation. Quality is part of every decision of the business.

Training, recruitment, expansion, design, marketing, and investment decisions all have implications for quality. Quality must be considered in these decisions. Quality must be considered all of the time.

Quality is not a function in its own right; it is part of every function. It must become part of the automatic thinking of every line manager, in all decisions.

For a business to achieve quality requires everyone in the business, and the suppliers to the business, to believe that quality is the only way to go. Achieving quality is about total commitment and total involvement.

Techniques, systems and policies are all tools that enable management to focus on quality and achieve quality. But the achievement of quality is not about techniques, it is not about systems, it is not about policies. Achieving quality is about hearts and minds. The best systems in the world will not by themselves achieve quality. Policies alone are just words. Techniques are just tools. Quality is about attitudes, values, outlook and philosophy.

If a business has prioritized the pursuit of output over quality, cost over value, short-term over long-term, then the achievement of quality requires a transformation in the business. The management of the business must change their whole thinking. They must alter their attitudes and values.

Quality is so vital to a business that its achievement justifies these changes. From the top to the bottom everyone needs to know that quality is the number one priority, and to know it they need to see management demonstrate it.

The quality performance of a business is so public, so well known to the employees, that for quality to be achieved, management has to take the lead. If they sense it is a paper exercise, management will not win their hearts and minds. Management will fail.

Quality is achievable in any business. The achievement may not be easy, but it is worthwhile. Managing the achievement is the most worthwhile role in a business. It results in increased profits, improved morale, more committed customers and improved standing in the marketplace. What could be more worthwhile for management to achieve? What could be more disastrous for management to fail to achieve?

WHEN IS QUALITY ACHIEVED?

SUMMARY

The journey to quality is a never-ending journey. As improvements are achieved new horizons are seen and new goals have to be established. This is the nature of quality, our customers' expectations are continually changing and if we are to continue to delight these customers our performance has to continually improve.

Along the quality road there are definable milestones. These provide businesses with a measure of their progress along the road. Some of these measures are internal and provide management with evidence of the progress down the road. Some of the measures are external and provide opportunities to demonstrate to employees, customers and society the progress that has been achieved.

These measures have value in their own right, but they have the danger that they can become the quality goal. They have greatest value when they are part of a genuine determination by the whole business, management, stakeholders and employees, to achieve quality.

Quality is really about an attitude of mind. It is about accepting that there are always ways to improve and that these need to be actively sought out and taken as opportunities and not problems. If someone says they can improve no more, it says more about their attitude than the service they are providing. Quality is a never-ending journey through continual improvement.

THE STARTING POINT
As with all journeys the journey to quality starts with the decision to set off. Once taken, commitment to the journey gradually increases. As it becomes known that

a business has started down the road, its customers, employees and even the rest of society expect the journey to continue. They are looking for evidence that progress is being made and they evaluate the business through that evidence.

The starting point is the commitment to make the journey. As there is no end, then there can be no cast-iron guarantees about the journey. Logic may indicate that it is a worthwhile journey to take, those who are making the journey may say it is the only journey to take, customers may want you to take the journey, but that does not make the decision a foregone conclusion.

Every business is unique. Every business has to make its own decision, its own commitment to the journey. It has to be a real commitment for it not to be abandoned at the first sign of pressure. It has to be taken by the executive management of the business and be believed by them to be the right journey and a viable journey. They have to guide the business along the road, they have to understand the nature of the journey, the bene-fits it will bring and the challenges that will need to be overcome.

The executive management of the business have to make the commitment to the journey. Without their hearts and minds it will not happen. The commitment has to be far more than a paper exercise. It has to be based on a belief that it is the only way for their business to succeed. They have to commit to putting quality first, each day, every day. This is a commitment for them and of them.

It requires more than commitment, it requires involve-ments. If they leave it as a commitment that the business will make the journey, then it will probably be a fruit-less journey. They have to be involved in making it happen, be at the wheel, looking at progress and adjusting the course. Everyone needs to see that they mean it, by their actions and not just by their words. This is the commitment that is needed to start the journey. The achievement of this commitment is the starting point of the achievement of quality.

ALTERNATIVE ROUTES

The journey to quality may be one without end, but it is not one without a map. In fact there are numerous maps, each based on the journeys of different businesses. This in itself is one of the problems with the journey and it is all too easy to use it as an excuse for not setting off.

In making any journey it is useful to have, at the outset, defined methods of measuring progress. A journey without measures can become a journey without purpose, a meandering drifting journey, generally heading in the right direction, but with no measure of progress.

In choosing the route it is useful to decide on the measures to judge the progress. There are currently three commonly accepted measures, each looking at a different aspect of progress. These measures are separate, but there is considerable synergy between them. They are the 'Systems Approach' with ISO 9000 as the accepted measure, the 'People Approach' with Investors in People becoming the accepted measure and the 'Financial Approach' with a measure of quality costs being the accepted measure.

These approaches are not mutually exclusive, in fact the converse is true. Using any one of the three will move a business along the path of the other approaches. Using all three approaches takes advantage of the synergy between them and provides an holistic approach that maximizes the benefits.

These three approaches and their three measures have the advantage that any business, given the right level of commitment, can achieve the measures. They can all succeed. Success brings recognition, and recognition helps quality as it builds a pride in the business and justifies the commitment.

There are a set of other measures of success in the form of Quality Awards. These are generally based on the assessment of business performance with respect to quality to determine the 'best' business. They measure performance across all functions of the business and provide an holistic view of the business.

Each business is unique, and hence one should expect each journey to be unique. Some businesses already have strong inspection departments and need a realignment of thinking. Some may have excellent customer care programmes, but do not measure their performance. Some may have formalized systems, but do not involve their staff in decision making.

Different management philosophies and priorities can have an affect on management thinking. Those with a financial background may favour a quality costs route, those with a more technical background may favour a systems approach and those from human resources a people approach. All approaches have validity, and for the complete journey all will be necessary. It is more a matter of deciding which approach to use to start.

ISO 9000 – A SYSTEMS MILESTONE
ISO 9000 is a series of International Standards that addresses quality systems. Their origin can be traced back to early military standards which were adopted as the British Standard, BS 5750, in 1979. This standard was the most widely-read British Standard of all time, and became an International Standard in 1987.

The International Standards Organization is composed of member countries and its aim is to establish harmonized standards throughout the world. Each standard that it produces has no authority in itself, but is open for adoption by member nations. The ISO 9000 series of standards has been adopted by over 80 nations, which include all the industrialized nations of the world.

In the ISO 9000 series there are several standards which provide guidance for different types of businesses, and there are three assessment standards. These are ISO 9001, ISO 9002, and ISO 9003. Each of these assessment standards defines a similar level of requirement, but they are applicable for different types of businesses. The standards are in an hierarchical structure with the requirements of ISO 9003 being included in ISO 9002, which again are included in ISO 9001.

If a business is responsible for the design of the product or service it provides then it is appropriate for it to apply ISO 9001. If a business provides a service or makes products to established designs then ISO 9002 is the appropriate standard. If a business provides an inspection or test service only then it may apply ISO 9003. Whichever standard a business decides is appropriate to its operations the method of assessment is the same.

Each of these assessment standards defines aspects and controls that it is considered need to be present in a quality system to ensure that the customers' needs and expectations are met. They do not define how a business is to be organized, but rather indicate what is necessary for good control. How this is achieved is left to the business.

To prepare for assessment an organization has to document its quality system. This need not be an over-bureaucratic task, indeed the less paperwork involved the better. It needs to start with a definition of the quality policy and then describe the processes used by the business to achieve quality. The level of this documentation needs to be appropriate for the skills, training and education of the employees. If you can demonstrate that they know the details of a process the level of documentation can be minimal.

Once the documentation is in place, the implementation needs to be demonstrated through a formal internal audit programme. The results of this programme have to be reviewed by the executive management and used as a means to improve the system and its implementation.

When the audits and reviews show that the system is functioning efficiently and is in line with the documentation then assessment can take place.

The assessments for ISO 9000 are conducted by independent Certification Bodies. These bodies should be accredited by the National Authority of the country in which they operate. In the UK this is the National Accreditation Council of Certification Bodies (NACCB). This ensures their competence.

The assessment against the standard is done in three stages. At the first stage it is confirmed that the documentation describing the quality system indicates that all of the requirements of the standard have been addressed. This may be done on site or at the office of the Certification Body. If any shortfalls are identified then these are drawn to the attention of the applicant for corrective action.

At the second stage the business is visited by a team from the Certification Body and it is confirmed that the system is operating as described and that all of the requirements of the standard have been addressed. Again shortfalls may be identified. If the shortfalls are of a minor nature then, on the basis of the assessment, registration to the standard is recommended. This is subject to the understanding that the shortfalls are addressed. If the shortfalls are numerous or of a major nature the recommendation may be deferred until a second visit to confirm that suitable actions have been taken.

If it is found that there are fundamental problems with the quality system then registration is not recommended.

In all cases the recommendation for registration has to be endorsed by the Board of the Certification Body. In practice this is a formality.

The third stage of the registration process is the ongoing surveillance of the system by the Certification Body. This involves visits to the business at approximately six-monthly intervals when different aspects of the quality system are reassessed. Shortfalls identified at these visits are required to be corrected to maintain registration. In the event of a total breakdown of the system it may be recommended that the registration is withdrawn.

As the quality system covers most areas of the business, the majority of employees are involved in its achievement. They are involved in achieving registration, it provides them with recognition and gives them a level of pride in the achievement.

The achievement of the standard should not be taken as a static milestone along the journey. Working the system improves quality. While the standard does not change assessors look for improvement in the operation of the system.

All ISO standards are reviewed every five years. The current standard was issued in 1994 and the next revision will be in place before the end of the century. The next revision is expected to make the standard more comprehensive and to introduce more measures of total quality. This new standard will still be a milestone on the road, but it is expected to be further along the road.

INVESTORS IN PEOPLE – A PEOPLE MILESTONE

The greatest asset of any business is its people. It is people who make the difference between a deserted mill and a thriving factory, an empty office and a profitable business. It is people who make the difference between profit and loss, it is people who provide products and services that delight customers, it is people who provide quality.

The importance of people in business is recognized in the standard **Investors in People**. This standard is a UK national standard operated through the Training and Enterprise Councils (TECs) in England and Wales and in Scotland through Local Enterprise Companies (LECs). Its objective is to promote and recognize investment in the training of people employed in the UK economy.

The standard defines 24 assessment indicators which are grouped into four areas. In essence the standard requires an employer to make and implement a public commitment to develop all employees to achieve the business objectives.

The public commitment is the starting point of the **Investors in People** process and must involve communication with the employees. The implementation of this commitment needs to go through defined steps which start with the development of a business plan which, along with other business objectives, must address the contribution to the business of the employees. This is followed by reviews of the training and development needs of the employees, the development of suitable training plans, training actions to meet the identified needs and evaluation of the effectiveness of the training on both a personal and business level.

The **Investors in People** standard and assessment process is operated by the TECs and LECs. It is only through them that recognition can be achieved. They promote the standard as a means of promoting training, and different TECs and LECs provide different levels of support to organizations seeking recognition. This may be in the form of financial support or expertise, or a combination of both.

To achieve recognition a business is required to start by making a public commitment. This must come from the chief executive of the business and is usually in the form of a letter to the TEC or LEC making a commitment to pursue the standard. The commitment is usually linked with an action plan prepared with the TEC or LEC indicating how and when the standard will be achieved.

Following on from the commitment, the business is required to develop a business plan that sets out goals for the business and considers how the employees will contribute to the achievement of these goals. If this business plan identifies quality as a goal, then the **Investors in People** standard becomes an explicit quality standard and its achievement a quality milestone. The implementation of the employee training and development plans and the assessment of their effectiveness take the business through to meeting the requirements of the standard.

Many of these requirements may already be met by the

business, and indeed those who have already achieved ISO 9000 should have the necessary training and development procedures in place.

A major car distribution group had sound staff development and training procedures. These were supplemented by training schemes operated in conjunction with car manufacturers for the various franchises.

Each dealership had a business plan which addressed the operating activities, but did not link these to training and development issues. Making this link improved the focus of the group on their employees, their major asset, and enabled them to achieve Investors in People. It provided them with evidence that they were a quality company.

Having met the requirements of the standard, to achieve registration to the standard it is necessary for the business to prepare a 'Portfolio of Evidence'. The portfolio demonstrates how each of the 24 indicators is being met by the business and should contain copies of existing documents that illustrate this. The evidence may be in the form of the business plan, training and development plans and records, minutes of meetings and evidence of training which has taken place. It is not intended that there should be a need to create evidence, only to copy and collate it into one document for assessment purposes.

The only additional requirement in the portfolio is a summary showing which items of evidence meet which of the indicators. As the standard is holistic in nature the indicators involve some considerable overlap, and one item of evidence could support several indicators.

The portfolio is submitted to the TEC who arrange for

an independent assessor to review and report on its contents. This may involve a visit to the business, but this is not a requirement of the process. The report is passed to the applicant and actions may be taken as appropriate.

The assessment involves a visit to the business when the validity of the portfolio is assessed through interviews across the business. As the standard is about commitment, emphasis is placed on the attitudes of executive management to the principles of the standard.

On the basis of the visit the assessor prepares a report and makes a recommendation to the TEC or LEC. They then decide whether to recognize the business as an **Investor in People**. This decision is not a formality and local knowledge of the business may be used to supplement the contents of the assessor's report.

Once recommended for registration the business is expected to continue to follow the policies introduced to gain the standard, but re-assessment is only on a three-year cycle.

Meeting the standard is about the recognition of the importance of people to the success of a business, that their training and development is the way to take the business forward. If the business plan addresses quality then the commitment to quality will be assessed. If the training and development plans address the improvement of the processes used by the business, then the training for quality and its effectiveness will be assessed. It may be argued that this is not explicitly about quality, but certainly those who are travelling down the quality road can use the standard as a guide on that journey and its achievement as a milestone on the way.

QUALITY COSTS – A FINANCIAL MILESTONE
The American quality guru, Philip Crosby, maintains that the only measure of quality is the cost of quality,

the cost of not doing it right first time. This is clearly a valid measure of performance, and can therefore be used as a measure of progress along the quality road. As the figures are of a continuous nature it provides more of a series of milestones as the costs are reduced.

The measurement of the cost of quality can provide justification for the journey and evidence of progress. It is a measure that is internal and varies from business to business. To set targets and allow for comparisons between businesses the percentage of the cost of quality to the cost of sales is often used. This is meaningful as it indicates the percentage of the turnover of the business that is wasted correcting things that could, and should, have been done right first time.

When the measurement of the cost of quality is first undertaken by a business it is not unusual to find that the cost exceeds 20 per cent of the sales turnover. In some industries it is even higher. When using the figure as a mark of progress down the quality road the absolute value of this figure is not as important as the reduction of it.

Using the measure of the cost of quality to indicate progress down the quality road provides objective evidence of what has been achieved and its value to the business. Whilst many businesses are reluctant to publicize the figures as it exposes previous inefficiencies, when the savings are seen they provide justification for the journey.

An automotive component manufacturer made an estimate of the cost of quality and found it to be 22 per cent of sales turnover. It was decided that the financial controller should report the figure monthly to the board and indicate the 'top ten' causes. Plans were drawn up to address the 'top

ten' and slowly they were solved. Other issues came into the 'top ten' to replace them, but all the time the cost of quality was being driven down. After three years it reached five per cent, but the drive goes on.

There is a danger that having moved from 20 per cent down to less than say five per cent a level of complacency sets in and questions are asked as to how much further it can be expected to fall. In practice it has been found that continual improvement means just that and the figure is pushed lower and lower. Leading quality companies are reporting figures of less than 0.5 per cent, from a start at over 20 per cent. The implications to the profitability of those concerns is clearly immense.

On the journey it is often found that plateaux are encountered where little or no progress is made in reducing the cost. Sometimes increases are even detected, though these can often be attributed to improvements in the method of collecting the data. This does not mean the journey should be abandoned or the measurements ceased. In fact the opposite is true as once stability is achieved the opportunity to use statistical methods to identify deviations becomes available.

The cost of quality is a measure of the journey which has meaning to the management and stakeholders of the business. It is truly objective and independent of outside standards or assessors. It provides a continual measure of the progress rather than a single milestone. These aspects make it the most attractive measure for many.

QUALITY AWARDS – AN ACCOLADE FOR THE BEST
Over the last decade many prizes have been introduced for the organization that is considered to have achieved the highest quality of performance. These prizes started

in Japan, moved into the USA and are now to be found in Europe. They may be on a local, national, or indeed a European basis, but as with any competition there is only a limited number of winners.

Whilst the organizers may not see them as such these prizes are based on competitions. While quality of performance is judged in these competitions, it is not just about meeting the criteria but more about being able to demonstrate that you are better than the others.

Whilst competitions can provide evidence of exceptional performance, they require resources to be allocated to 'compete', and 'failure' is inevitable for most. Everyone can train and cover a hundred metres at their own pace, but there is only one Olympic gold medal winner.

The initial rounds of the competitions are normally based on submissions from the competitors. They are required to submit details of their performance and show how it compares with others in their industrial sector, with improvement in performance being a key factor. This benchmarking of one competitor against others is a key feature of the competitions.

The final founds involve visits to the competitors by the assessors when the facts in the written submissions are verified. Further evidence of performance may be sought.

The winners do not achieve a definitive standard, but have only been found best when judged against the others using the declared criteria. Unlike ISO 9000 and Investors in People, competitions are a variable standard and are not universally available. Winning the prize is dependent not only on the quality of performance but also on being able to present the facts well.

This is very much a management task, and some competitors take on teams specifically to prepare the submissions. This work is extraneous to the achievement of quality, and could indeed detract from it. But it is a task which obliges the business to analyse its own performance, compare that performance with others, and look hard at what it finds.

These results have value, even if they do not win. They provide information on how the business is performing and provide benchmarks for the journey along the quality road.

The process of preparing a submission for an award has value in itself. The examination and rating of the performance of the business has value and most organizations use the assessment criteria to learn about themselves; to see what they need to address to improve their performance. They determine where they would score low, and then action can be taken to increase the rating. Whether a company goes forward to enter for the award or not it will still have gained from the process.

The winners of the prizes certainly see them as a measure of their achievement of quality. Much publicity follows the prize and is used to promote the business. The prizes are a milestone along the road to quality, but they are a milestone which cannot be achieved by all.

IT IS BETTER TO TRAVEL THAN TO ARRIVE

If the journey to quality is a journey without end, then literally speaking it is impossible to arrive. In spite of this the journey is worthwhile, and many consider it to be the best road to travel down.

While travelling the road to quality a business is continually looking for opportunities to improve. These opportunities may arise from customer complaints, reject material, faulty parts or any other failure to 'do it right first time'. If these opportunities are taken, then there should be fewer things going wrong. The emphasis moves from dealing with problems to correcting their causes and seeking to prevent them recurring.

By establishing sound quality systems the ability to delegate effectively is increased, communication is improved and knowledge is shared. Work can be given to others in the confidence that there is a system which controls and makes it happen.

The training and development of all of the employees to the limit of their abilities and potential provides a business with an increase in resources. If this is used then the benefits to the business are enormous. The harnessing of human resources allows for growth of the business and of the staff. They become more satisfied with their work and take a greater pride in it. They like to work in a quality company where their work is valued, and this is reflected in their performance.

These factors all make the quality road the best road to travel. It is a road on which one encounters less conflict and more delighted customers. The profits of those who travel this road are improved and long-term security is more likely. This reduces conflict and the stress and strain of managing a business, and makes it the optimum road to travel.

FURTHER READING

About the philosophical meaning of Quality:
Pirsig, R.M., *Zen and the Art of Motorcycle Maintenance,*
Bantam Books, New York, 1974

About the work of Dr Deming:
Neave, H.R., *The Deming Dimension,*
SPC Press, Tennessee, 1990

Mann, N., *The Keys to Excellence,*
Mercury, London, 1989

About Total Quality and Quality Techniques:
Oakland, J.S., *Total Quality Management,*
Heinemann, Oxford, 1989

Ishikawa, K., *What is Total Quality Control?,*
Prentice Hall, New Jersey, 1985

Wille, E., *Quality: Achieving Excellence,*
Century Business, London, 1992

About Customer Service:
Johns, T., *Perfect Customer Care,*
Arrow Business Books, London, 1994

Taylor, L.K., *Quality: Total Customer Service,*
Century Business, London, 1993

About Quality Systems and ISO 9000:
Owen, B.D., and Malkovitch P., *Understanding the
 Value of ISO 9000 Registration,*
SPC Press, Tennessee, 1995

Owen, B.D., Cothran, T. and Malkovitch P., *Achieving ISO 9000 Registration,*
SPC Press, Tennessee, 1994

About Statistical Process Control:
Wheeler, D.J., *Understanding Variation,*
SPC Press, Tennessee, 1994

Wheeler, D.J. and Chambers, *Understanding Statistical Process Control,*
SPC Press, Tennessee, 1992

About the Cost of Quality:
Crosby, P.B., *Quality is Free,*
McGraw–Hill Book Co, New York, 1979

Groucock, J.M., *The Cost of Quality,*
Pitman Publishing, London, 1974

About Quality Circles:
Chaudhry-Lawton, R., Lawton, R., Murphy, K., and Terry, A., *Quality: Change Through Teamwork,*
Century Business, London, 1993

Robson, M., *Quality Circles Members Handbook,*
Gower, London, 1982

THE PERFECT BUSINESS PLAN

Ron Johnson

A really professional business plan is crucial to success. This book provides a planning framework and shows you how to complete it for your own business in 100 easy to follow stages.

Business planning will help you to make better decisions today, taking into account as many of the relevant factors as possible. A carefully prepared business plan is essential to the people who will put money into the business, to those who will lend it money, and above all to the people who carry out its day to day management.

£5.99 Net in UK only.

ISBN 0-7126-5524-7

THE PERFECT NEGOTIATION

Gavin Kennedy

The ability to negotiate effectively is a vital skill required in business and everyday situations.

Whether you are negotiating over a business deal, a pay rise, a difference of opinion between manager and staff, or the price of a new house or car, this invaluable book, written by one of Europe's leading experts in negotiation, will help you to get a better deal every time, and avoid costly mistakes.

£5.99 Net in UK only.

ISBN 0-7126-5465-8

PERFECT PR

Marie Jennings

We are all communicators – all the time. It is vitally important to consider what we are communicating, and whether or not we are being effective. Public relations is increasingly recognized as an important business tool, but it is a personal tool as well. Understanding PR and how to make it work for you as well as for your company will help you get what you want from your life.

Perfect PR helps you to examine yourself as a communicator. It gives a bird's-eye view of PR, describes the various techniques involved, and shows you how to make the most of them.

Covering PR for individuals, companies, products and charities, this is the perfect book for anyone who has a job of promotion to do, whatever the subject.

£5.99 Net in UK only.

ISBN 0–09–950811–7

PERFECT MARKETING

Louella Miles

Every company wants sustainable growth and over the years it has been marketing that has helped them to achieve it. Yet marketing suffers a muddled identity, often confused with selling and advertising.

This book sets the record straight. It looks at marketing as a whole and at each of its constituent parts, offering guidance on what can be achieved realistically and how to measure results. It examines the industry of the 90s, the impact of new technology, the role of innovation and how marketers can plan not just for survival but for growth.

£5.99 Net in the UK only.

ISBN 0–09–950521–5

PERFECT DECISIONS

Andrew Leigh

Everybody has to make decisions, and this book gives a wealth of tips and information on how to make them more effectively. So much in our lives and careers depends on taking the right turning when we are faced with a choice of actions; *Perfect Decisions* helps you to minimize the guesswork and demystifies the decision making process, giving you the confidence to weigh up the pros and cons and pick the best course of action either on your own or as part of a team.

£5.99 Net in UK only.

ISBN 0–7126–5902–1

PERFECT RECRUITMENT

David Oates and Viv Shackleton

Organizations are only as good as the people who run
them and there are few more important management
tasks than recruiting the right staff to secure progress
and success. There are a battery of techniques for
assessing job applications – such as psychometric testing, assessment centres and graphology – and opinions
vary as to their effectiveness. This book evaluates the
different ways to arrive at a shortlist and to select the
best person to fill a vacancy.

£5.99 Net in UK only.

ISBN 0–09–937921–X